PRACTICAL
ALCHEMY

PRACTICAL ALCHEMY

A Guide to the Great Work

BRIAN COTNOIR

Introduction by James Wasserman
Foreword by Robert Allen Bartlett

WEISER BOOKS

This edition first published in 2021 by Weiser Books, an imprint of
Red Wheel/Weiser, LLC
With offices at:
65 Parker Street, Suite 7
Newburyport, MA 01950
www.redwheelweiser.com

ISBN: 978-1-57863-747-8.
Library of Congress Cataloging-in-Publication Data available upon request.

Cover design by Kathryn Sky-Peck
Cover art: The true principles of all things, from "The works of Jacob Behmen,
the Teutonic theosophe," by William Law, 1764/Getty Research Institute,
Los Angeles, USA/Bridgeman Images
Interior photos/images by Sesthasak Boonchai and Susan McCann
Typeset in Sabon

Printed in the United States of America
IBI
10 9 8 7 6 5 4 3 2 1

Disclaimer

The practice of alchemy involves working with chemical supplies and techniques that
may be dangerous or fatal if done improperly. Every effort has been made in the text
to encourage the practitioner both to use proper safety precautions in the experiments
suggested and to equip him- or herself with additional formal training in laboratory procedures. In the case of herbal preparations, consult with a physician before ingesting any
herbs or tinctures discussed herein. The author, editor, and publisher disclaim any and all
responsibility for accidents or problems resulting from improper use of this material. This
book is intended for informational purposes only.

If the fool would persist in his folly, he would become wise.
PROVERBS OF HELL, WILLIAM BLAKE

This book is dedicated:

To RC, who taught me to read and that curiosity may have killed the cat but, "satisfaction brought him back."

To FC, who taught me that there is nothing supernatural, only natural laws we don't understand.

To EW, for grammar, grace, and beauty.

To the dakinis ML, LC, SC, SF, MM, and ST, who gave with eyes, heart, and hands—light, love, and protection.

Sororis mysticae meae, můj mlok LV.

To my teachers too numerous to mention.

To all those who have gone before. and
To the one who comes after.

It is my hope that only good may come of this.

ACKNOWLEDGMENTS

I would like to thank:

James Wasserman for the opportunity to present this "report from the front" and for his patience and faith in me; Sandra Feist, Ina L.Chow, and Maria Levitsky, for their corrections and suggestions; Lucille Carra, Ellen Wood, and Lenka Vařekova for their general feedback and encouragement; Sesthasak Boonchai and Susan McCann for the book's illustrations; and finally Tover for lending me his mom.

CONTENTS

FOREWORD

If you are new to the study of alchemy, or even if you've been around it for awhile and need some additional guidance or inspiration, this is the book for you.

Where does one begin the study of such a mysterious art? A simple internet search can net you millions of hits; it could take years just to sort out the true from the false. You see, that has always been a problem with the study of alchemy; it has a long history of being presented through a unique terminology (like any other science or art), which is cryptic and obscure if you don't possess certain keys.

We have so much information available to us today; at the push of a few buttons I can view documents across all of recorded history. A book I never thought I'd see because only one or two exist? No problem; now I have a digitized photocopy of it for study.

Now, here's the rub; with alchemy being so mysterious and obscure, there are many who use the "wondrous secrets of alchemy" to present their version of the story, and suddenly, we are beset with pet theories, aliens, Atlanteans, dangerous chemistry, and government conspiracies. It is easy to get pulled into a labyrinth from which it may take considerable time to "unlearn" and in some cases, survive.

The famous Swiss physician and alchemist, Paracelsus, said that alchemy is the art of separating the pure from the impure, the true from the false, and that is what my friend and author of this book, Brian Cotnoir, has done for us concisely.

Within the pages of this book you will find a reliable guide on who and what to study and where to delve even deeper if you are truly interested in understanding the Sacred Art that is alchemy, not just from a theoretical and philosophic viewpoint but from its practical applications as well.

How do I know this to be true? I have personally explored alchemy for the past fifty years (yes, there's that much to explore) starting in a time when information about alchemy, especially of a practical nature, was hard to find. And yet, if I had such a book as this and knew it was reliable and true to the Alchemical Art, my searches would have been accelerated beyond measure. I would have known to study such things as Aristotle's Physics and Metaphysics because these ideas held sway all through the "Golden Age of Alchemy," and the terminology and concepts presented are what the ancient writers of alchemy were referring to. So when the alchemist Petrus Bonus of Ferrara, in his work *New Pearl of Great Price*, says, "The Philosopher's Stone is the Form of Gold," it takes on a whole new sense considering Aristotle's ideas on Matter and Form.

Our author and guide presents us with another important subject for close scrutiny: Humoral Medicine, the medicine of Roman physician Galen and later expanded by Avicenna. Again, these are the concepts and language the early alchemists thought in. Now, if I come across an alchemical formula that says, "This medicine excites the Animal Spirit," I will know that it is not a super aphrodisiac or that I may change into a werewolf, but that it is a liver tonic.

This book touches all the bases you need to delve into deeply in order to gain entrance to the alchemical mysteries. The charts, tables, and line drawings are all very well done and deserve close study.

And don't even get me started on practical matters in alchemy. As a professional chemist, this has been my own area of investigation over the years, and I can tell you flat out that the instructions given in this book are clear and true and can lead you safely into the incredible world of Spagyric and Alchemical Medicines. You can do this yourself and, in so doing, the Alchemical Work becomes elucidated all the more; working with Nature, you can hold the alchemical principles in your hand and create medicines that are effective and sometimes miraculous in effect.

Many people think they can't do this kind of work because they don't have a laboratory and chemical glassware. Setting up an alchemical lab in your house can be a little scary, if you are new to it, but this author offers a very reasonable list of equipment to gather and sound advice on setup, care, and maintenance. Start off slow and gather your "tools" as needed; many can be found inexpensively in thrift stores.

Finally, we come to the bibliography; this is excellent. If you are serious about the study of alchemy in all of its aspects, I would recommend looking into each of the references provided with great care. Most are readily available from the internet and will lead you to find other related works. As the alchemists would say, "One book opens another."

I wish I had such a guide fifty years ago; I heartily recommend that you buy this book and use it as a true and faithful guide through the labyrinth of alchemy.

—ROBERT ALLEN BARTLETT
author of *Real Alchemy: A Primer of Practical Alchemy*

INTRODUCTION

It is a distinct pleasure to introduce this brilliant book on alchemy by my friend Brian Cotnoir. Well over thirty years ago, Brian walked into Samuel Weiser's Bookstore in New York City where I then worked. I was twenty-four, Brian seventeen. His utter seriousness of purpose struck me then and remains my assessment of him to this day.

Brian describes this book as the one he wishes had been available when he began his lifelong study of alchemy. I challenge any reader to find a more succinct and clear guide to this science and art. Brian begins with the Work. Totally eschewing what I have long considered to be the superficial psychological interpretation of modern deconstructionists driven to trivialize anything beyond their own limited view of reality, this book begins by defining exactly what alchemy is, and how it can best be approached by one who seeks to learn its secrets. Laboratory techniques and equipment are then discussed in an earnest and serious manner that only highlights the intensity of the historical overview he next provides.

The reader becomes immediately aware that we are tracing the footsteps of historical heroes who risked life and limb to plumb the secret depths of Sacred Nature. And who did so while enflamed in prayer. Thereby did these giants give rise to modern chemistry and physics. Yet something was lost in the process. The failing of the eighteenth-century Enlightenment movement was its embrace of hyperrationalism. The empirical imperative turned True Science on its head. The scientist/adept was forced to deny the sense of humility and wonder that his research engendered. The love for the Creator who fashioned the miracle of matter was relegated to the superstitions of the past.

The author proceeds to a thorough overview of the theoretical universe of the practicing alchemist. Why should a process performed on matter redound to the spiritual benefit of the operator? And how does an action performed on one thing transform it into another thing entirely? Can someone really turn lead into gold? As Brian writes:

> By finishing what nature had started by separating, purifying, and balancing the three principles and recombining them, lead could be completed and perfected, transmuted into gold.

With little delay, Brian plunges the reader into the actual alchemical work itself. Beginning with the Herbal Work, you will be working with formulas and heat sources, chemicals and labware. Instead of the instantaneous gratification our culture expects from television and email, you will be directed to undertake works of the alchemical art whose stages are measured in months. You will be ever reminded that prayer and mantra, meditation and spiritual integrity, along with grace, will be the necessary concomitants of your work.

By the time you have come through the Herbal Work, you will have developed the techniques and skills to begin the next level. For this book now takes the reader directly into the more complex and dangerous Mineral Work. The author suggests you consider attending a class in laboratory techniques at a local college if you wish to gain the most benefit from his writings. You will now be entering that sacred space in which one's magical implements become the beaker and burner, the flask and scales.

Will you personally manage to transform lead into gold? If such a thing is possible (and I believe it is) and if you are willing to invest the effort required to succeed in such work, I can think of no better book to send you on your way. And if you have already read other books on alchemy and been mystified, confused, or disappointed, get ready for a transformative experience. For here you will encounter a masterful guide to the Path of the Wise. And its excellent bibliography will provide valuable direction for your continued journey.

—JAMES WASSERMAN

PREFACE

The purpose of this book is to provide an entryway into the world of alchemy, its fundamental principles and practices. It is the sort of guide I wish I had had when I started my investigations many years ago. It is my hope that this small endeavor will be helpful to those who wish to further explore alchemy.

The work will provide some basic, but essential, theory. It presents a framework that should be developed (or discarded) as your own work on the alchemical path develops. To actually practice alchemy, the techniques encountered in cooking, brewing, and building fires are all that are really necessary at first, and much of alchemy can be done using only these techniques. Some of the more advanced work requires knowledge and experience with high temperatures and some very toxic and caustic materials, and to this end I would highly recommend a few practical chemistry classes and perhaps some metalworking classes in order to learn safe techniques and handling of materials. However, to begin, much of the basic work and the preparation for more advanced alchemical work can be done with the aforementioned skills.

The outline of the procedures, theories, and practices presented here is a distillation from my notes of the various work plans, dreams, and meditations that developed over time from my own research and experimentation. These practices are some of the key works within an overall work. All have been culled from primary sources and have been somewhat standardized against the practices of such contemporary alchemists as Archibald Cockren, Alexander von Bernus, Augusto Pancaldi, Frater Albertus, Manfred Junius, and Jean Dubuis, who, on the whole, have a practice based on the alchemy and writings of Paracelsus (1493–1541).

So what is meant by alchemy?

The central concept in alchemy is transmutation: the fundamental change of one thing into another, from a grosser, impure state to a more refined, balanced, and pure state. This is to be understood on multiple levels—physically, spiritually, and symbolically.

In the worldview of alchemy, each thing in all of creation is a dynamic mix of body, spirit, and soul. A thing's physicality is only one aspect of that thing. The heart, for instance, is not only the physical pump in our chest but a living symbol of spirituality in a variety of aspects, all simultaneous with one another. For an alchemist, the heart is the physical, mental, and spiritual center of the person. Through the study of nature, which is a divine expression of God, also referred to as a theophany of God, one can discover God.

By opening up dense matter, obstructions are loosened and light begins to stream through. The ascent to God through God's creation is accomplished by understanding and working; step by step, rung by rung, the ladder is ascended. This is alchemy. This is what the alchemist seeks in the world: a way to open a body—a means by which the dense, solid, and heavy becomes solvent, fluid, and light. Once matter is purified and open to the intent of the alchemist and to the grace of God, transmutation can take place. In fact, some views hold that the transmutation of base metals into gold is a reflection of the inner state of the alchemist. Others hold that it is the grace of God alone that allows transmutation to take place. Even so, the will of man, as St. Macarius of Egypt noted, "is an essential condition, for without it God does nothing." It is we who must move first.

And so, in working with matter, in reaching deep into its heart and changing it into a liquid, mirror-like, reflective state, alchemists work in the same way on themselves. Alchemy is much like iconography. An icon can be seen as a window showing the other, inner aspect of one's self. In creating an icon one is simultaneously working on the inner self, the inner icon.[1]

Both alchemy and iconography are *techniques* of gnosis[2]; they are stages and steps on the ladder of ascent. They are both paths for the artist. Both work with materials in the same manner—as living, symbolic material. The same may be said of music or poetry. In Greek, *poesis* means "to make." Alchemy was called *chrysopoeia* by the Greeks; literally, "gold-making." "Making" in this sense is the act of composition, the arrangement of elements, as in music. Perhaps a better translation of *poesis* would be "to compose" so that *chrysopoeia* becomes "gold-composing." One might consider the composition of words, that is, poetry, as an alchemical process. The poet takes the words (i.e., the material) from the dictionary, the rules (i.e., the techniques) from a book on grammar, and the poetic form (i.e., the process), and creates his work of art.

* * *

Though it may seem to begin with the inanimate, alchemy is a living process and is always working with living substances. Realize that what you are working with is alive and vibrant, and begin the work from there. As in most arts, the quality of the raw materials counts for a good deal of the rich and nuanced results to be had at the end of the various processes. Nonetheless, without the genius and effort of the alchemist/poet, we would still have nothing. The inner development of the alchemist is one of the fundamental keys to the process.

And so, it begins. *Ora, lege, lege, lege, relege, labora et invenies.* "Pray, read, read, read, reread, work, and you shall discover." This is the whole of the method.

What follows is the beginning of the work.

It is all process.

Mutus liber. Altus, 1677.

ORA

*There should be the invocation of God, flowing from the
depth of a pure and sincere heart, and a conscience which
should be free from all ambition, hypocrisy, and vice. . . .
Let constant prayer, to impart to you this Blessing, be the
beginning of your work.*[1]

—BASIL VALENTINE

Prayer (ora) is a key to the practice. It is not the prayer of
asking, "Please let it happen," but the prayer of aspiration,
of opening oneself up to Divinity and letting the light begin to
shine through the cracks. It is mindful recitation; it is *dhikr* or
recollection; it is the prayer of the heart.

Here is the prayer with which St. Albertus Magnus begins
his *Libellus de alchimia:*[2]

> "All wisdom is from the Lord God and hath been
> always with Him, and is before all time." Let whoever
> loves wisdom seek it in Him and ask it of Him, "who
> gives abundantly to all men, and does not reproach."
> For He is the height and the depth of all knowledge
> and the treasure houses of all wisdom, "since from
> Him and through Him and unto Him are all things":
> without Him nothing can be done; to Him be honor
> and glory forever. Amen.

All should commence with prayer, invocation, and a ded-
ication to the larger good. All should commence with good
intent. From there, invoke the grace of God, and dedicate the
fruit of your labor.

Overview of Alchemy

*But there is another science which is about the generation of
things from the elements, and from all inanimate things. . . .
This science is called "theoretical alchemy," which theorizes
about all inanimate things and about the generation of things
from the elements. There is in addition an operative and
practical alchemy, which teaches how to make noble metals,
colours, and many other things—better and more plentifully
by art than they are produced by nature.*

—Opus Tertium of Roger Bacon (1214–1294)

*A*lchemy is a word that has come to mean, in the popular
imagination, the changing of lead into gold. It is true that
many historical alchemists have pursued this goal, each with a
different motivation. For some, transmutation was an outward
sign—dramatic, yet only a sign of inner attainment; for others,
it was a demonstration of profound insight into nature. For
quite a few others, it was the dream of fast money. And for
some, it was a way to bring about peace and prosperity for the
many poor and sick.

Here is how some alchemists describe alchemy:

This science treats of the imperfect bodies of minerals,
and teacheth how to perfect them.[1]—Geber, thirteenth
century

Alchemy means: to carry to its end something that has
not yet been completed.[2]—Paracelsus, 1540

Alchemy is a science and art of making a fermentative
powder, which transmutes the imperfect metals into

gold, and which is a useful universal remedy for all the natural illnesses of man, of animals and of plants.[3]

—ANTOINE-JOSEPH PERNETY, 1758

The contemporary alchemist, Frater Albertus (1911–1984), spoke of alchemy as the "raising of vibrations,"[4] reflecting the view of Paracelsus that alchemy can transmute something "into its final substance and ultimate essence."[5]

The idea of transmutation goes back a long way in our history, starting with early metallurgy and craft initiation. Alchemy developed in a wide range of cultures, geographies, and times; like astrology, it grew out of a variety of factors coming together over time. The cosmopolitan crossroads of Alexandria were a particularly fertile meeting ground during the first few hundred years of our era. Here, Egyptian technology—both material and spiritual—encountered Greek philosophy, gnosticism, and hermeticism. From this potent mix, alchemy evolved. We see these influences in the writings of the Greek Zosimos of Panopoli (ca. 300 A.D.), for example. Alchemy then flowed from Hellenistic Egypt with the Greeks, via Orthodox monks, throughout such places as Egypt and Syria.

These monks were key in the transmission of Greek science and philosophy to Islam, translating texts from Greek into Arabic. One alchemical text, *Risalat Mariyanus al-Rahib al-hakim li-l-amir Khalid ibn Yazid,* is an account of just such a transmission of the wisdom of the Greek alchemists from a Syrian monk to Khalid ibn Yazid,[6] who supported the arts and sciences, including alchemy. This work (whose English title is translated as *The Epistle of Maryanus (Morienus), the Hermit and Philosopher to Prince Khalid ibn Yazid)* describes the teaching Morienus gave to Khalid concerning the elixir—that is, the Philosopher's Stone, the aim of the Great Work, that which can cure the illnesses of matter and men.

The art and science of alchemy rapidly advanced within the Islamic context, nurtured by Islam's embrace of both the natural sciences and gnosis. It was Jabir ibn Hayyan (721–815 A.D.) who developed Aristotle's idea of the formation of metals and minerals into a theory of Mercury and Sulphur, essential to understanding alchemy. The physician Ar-Razi (865–925 A.D.) developed an empirical system of classification for the materials used in alchemy that presaged modern chemistry. Islamic alchemy also had influences from India and China, but in the main it is of Hellenistic origin.

From the Islamic realms, alchemy came to Western Europe in February of 1144 with the translation of the *Risalat Mariyanus* from Arabic into Latin as *Liber de compositione alchimiae*. This was the beginning of the translation of many Arabic treatises into Latin. Jabir ibn Hayyan became known as Geber and Ar-Razi as Rhazes. The thirteenth-century European scholars Roger Bacon (1214–1294) and St. Albertus Magnus (1193–1280) are just two of the writers who reflect the next generation of alchemists—those who were working with and interpreting the translated Arabic texts. And so alchemy flowed through Europe. The most famous names of alchemists, real and imaginary, were Sir George Ripley, Paracelsus, Nicholas Flamel, Basil Valentine, Michael Maier, and Isaac of Holland. This marriage of philosophy and technology continued to develop until alchemy reached its peak in the mid-seventeenth century with Eirenaeus Philalethes. Sir Isaac Newton, himself a practicing alchemist, pointing his mind into matter as he had done with space, was perhaps both the last alchemist and the first physicist. By the end of the seventeenth century, alchemy had been entirely discredited. It wasn't until the late nineteenth and early twentieth century that alchemy experienced a revival of interest in its more spiritual, psychological, and healing aspects. The physical aspect, when presented at all, was strongly positioned within the context of either medicine or mystical initiation.

However, alchemy has always consisted of two aspects: the physical and the spiritual. Some early alchemists had a very strong orientation to the chemical aspects of the work, while others later took an almost purely mystical orientation. But both aspects were always present.

* * *

This brief sketch of the development of European alchemy provides a broad backdrop for the following discussions of alchemical theory and practice. Alchemy's journey is so varied that a definitive history has yet to be written. Familiarizing yourself with the history of alchemy will not be time wasted. If you pursue the alchemical path, you will find yourself at one time or another directly in front of a text whose process you would like to know, and whose insights you would like to understand. In the broadest terms, history can provide the keys to understanding.

In approaching the study and practice of alchemy, it is important to remember that there are as many alchemies as there are alchemists. Yes, they can be grouped by period, geographic region, philosophy, and religion, but at the heart of alchemy is the individual alchemist, his individual practice, and his particular writings. Which alchemist is speaking, and the context in which the text or practice exists, must be kept in mind while considering any text. Speaking even more broadly, context is everything.

For example, one alchemist will use the term "Green Lion" to mean stibnite, the mineral ore of the metal antimony, while another says that it is vitriol, a metallic sulphate salt. In his own context, each is correct. Try not to get lost in the dizzying array of terms, but instead to understand the function the term serves in that particular context. Do not assume that a term or symbol means the same thing from writer to writer, from period to period, or even in the works of a single writer. Once you understand what the symbol means for one alchemist for a specific process, it can be fruitful to examine other uses and meanings of the same symbol. When looking at a symbol across a variety of languages, countries, and cultures, we can perhaps at times see the symbol's more luminous center. And with this luminous center in mind, we can reapproach the symbol in its particular context and from there begin to see a deeper meaning for that term or symbol.

"**Liber enim librum aperit.**" *(One book opens another.)*
—RHAZES (AR-RAZI)

As we read a symbol within its context, so it is with a book. A more narrow interpretation of the phrase "one book opens another" is that one book is literally a key to another book. For instance, terms or materials used in one book to describe a process are defined and scattered throughout several books. This was a way of concealing from fools the precious knowledge of transmutation, but concealing it in a way that with some effort in reading and study, a process was given that even a fool could begin to understand.

For example, suppose it was a bread recipe that was being dispersed through three texts. In the first text the ingredients may be, "wheat, salt, the powder of expansion, and the crystals of the Sun." The second text may say, "The fruit of Ceres, a sweet solar powder, and salt." The third and final text may say, "the only thing necessary for the completion of the work is a water strengthened by the expansive dust collected from the grape and fed by the Sun." These three texts could be used together to interpret one another. We can interpret the ingredients to be wheat (Fruit of Ceres), salt, possibly yeast (powder of expansion/dust from the grape), possibly sugar (crystals of the Sun/sweet solar powder), and water. Typically the ingredients are not given fully or clearly in any one text—and, when finally worked out, there are still usually one or two questions remaining that only the actual attempt at the process will answer.

To truly glean the meaning from a particular work, you need to read a wide cross section of texts, and then go back to the original text and reread it. Each time this is done, a richer,

A Table of Chymicall & Philosophicall Characters wth their significations as they are vsually found in Chymicall Authors both printed & in manuscript

Saturne Lead	Balneü Mariæ	Mensis
	Balneü Vapory	Mercur: Jupiter
	Bene	Merc: Saturn
	Borax	Merc: Sublimat
Jupiter Tinne	Calcinare	
	Calx	Nota bene
	Calx viva	Nox
	Caly ovorum	
Mars Iron	Caput mortuu	Oleum
	Cæmentare	
	Cera	Præcipitare
Sol Gould	Christallum	Pulvis
	Cinis	Pulvis Latericius
	Cineres clavelati	Purificare
	Cinalar	Putrificare
	Coagulare	
Venus Copper	Cohobatio	Quinta Essentia
	Crocus Martis	Realgar
	Crocus Veneris	Regulus
	Æs vstum	Retorta
Mercury Quicksilver	Crucibulum	Sal comune
	Cucurbitum	Sal Alkali
		Sal Armoniac
		Sal Gemma
Luna Silver	Dies	Sal petra
	Digerere	Supo
	Dissolvere	Spiritus
	Distillar	Spiritus Vini
		Stratis super strata
	Filtrum	Solvere
Acetum	Fimus Equinus	Sublimare
Aceti distillat		Sulphur
Æs	Firune	Sulphur vivu
Aer	Flegma	Sulphur Philosophorü
Alembicus	Fluere	Sulphur nigu
Alumen		
Amalguma	Gumma	
Aunus		Tartar
Antimonium	Hora	Calx tartari
Aqua		Sal tartari
Aqua fortis		Talcum
Aqua Regis	Ignis	Terra
Aqua Vitæ	Ignis rota	Tigillum
Arena		Tutia
Arsenicam	Lapis calaminaris	
	Lapis	Vitriolum
Atramentü	Lutare	Vitrum
Amechakir	Lutum Sapientiæ	Viride æris
Au...	Magnes	Vrina
Libra	Marchsita	Johannes Worlidge
Libra, C... Scrupulus, Uncia, Ana	Materia Matrimonia	

Alchemical Signs. John Worlidge, sixteenth century

deeper understanding is reached and, in conjunction with practice, the heart of alchemy begins to reveal itself.

Other methods were used to conceal alchemy's secrets from fools. One was to use many names for one material—thus effectively burying its meaning in redundant noise. Another method was to repeat one or two of the materials over and over camouflaged in a variety of terms, so that a process that seems to need nine to ten materials really needs only three or four. Yet another way of disguising a true statement is to deny its truth after stating it. When a person blurts out some brutally honest but truthful comment to someone, one of the most common reactions of the speaker, on seeing the hurtful result of his words, will be to quickly try to ease, if not erase, their impact with assurances such as, "just kidding, I didn't mean it." The same is true in alchemical texts. When a writer declares that he will show the true way, then quickly follows up with a denial or disclaimer, such as "the mercury is not ordinary mercury but the mercury of the sages," implying something distinct from the usual meaning of the term, you must consider both meanings. Explore the possibility that either one may be correct, and analyze and work from there. At times you will see that in one text the confession is correct, while in a completely different text it is the denial that is correct.

Meaning was often disguised by use of signs. A sign is an arrangement of artifice. It is something thought up to represent a meaning such as many of the alchemical signs.

Signs are really a kind of shorthand since they point clearly and directly to what they mean. They need to be learned. Signs have also been used to hide meaning, and unless one has the key, the text is impossible to understand. The fifteenth-century *Voynich Manuscript* is an extreme example. Encrypted with images and signs, the manuscript remains silent to this day; none of our top cryptologists have been able to decode it.

A symbol, on the other hand, has a more spontaneous feeling and, when viewed or considered properly, tends to reveal rather than conceal. In fact, a symbol's purpose is to reveal meaning, not to conceal it. It is only a fog of our own making that obscures the symbol's light. A symbol is open to a more intuitive approach to understanding its meaning, and in alchemy it will often reveal the material or a method.

To fully understand the depth and reach of symbols, it is important to remember that alchemy is an art and is expressed through art. Study and consider the fine arts and literature of the period and location in relation to the text or author in question. In particular, study the depictions of myths, biblical stories, allegories, emblems, and heraldry, from which much alchemical imagery has its origins. This will also help you sift through some of the nonalchemical imagery and to realize that sometimes an elk is just an elk.

An excellent method of study is to reproduce the alchemical images by hand, whether by drawing, copying, or tracing. This forces you to make a careful study of the composition of the symbol as your eye takes in the detail and your hand gives it expression. As you do this, meditate on the various meanings and functions the symbol has and allow it to open to you.

I cannot emphasize enough the absolute necessity to read and re-read, contemplate, consider, and work in order to move along on the alchemical path.

The first gateway into the work is theory. Without theory, without our minds fully engaged in the work, the work just collapses into a pointless exercise, painting by numbers if you will—pretty in a kitschy sort of way, but of no real import. The alchemical theory to follow is an overview, but with enough detail to allow you to understand an alchemical text and to begin actual alchemical work.

Part One

THEORY

CHAPTER ONE

THE ASPECTS OF ALCHEMY

Empedocles says: "Nothing that is has a nature,
but only mixing and parting of the mixed, and nature is but
a name given them by men."[1]
—ARISTOTLE

B efore beginning any action one should have a clear mental
picture of it, the intent behind it, and how it will flow.
This is what is meant by theory. The word *theory* comes from
the Greek *theoria,* meaning "contemplation," or more exactly,
"divine vision." Theory is a mental laying-out of the view and
process. This is how theory should be approached—that is, the
world (or practice) described by the theory should be built up
mentally and visualized. Alchemical theory is actually a cosmology, a system for understanding how elements, events, and
phenomena evolve, interact, and dissolve—in short, how our
universe works. The cosmos or universe depicted by alchemical
theory is a rich one, with all aspects of creation interlinked. All
cosmology hinges on the level of focus and resolution. It is a
question of how much detail and precision we use to describe
whatever it is we are attempting to understand.

For example, say our universe is an island and we wish to
measure its circumference. Are we measuring the coastline in
meters or centimeters, yards or inches? What exactly do the
numbers mean? A coastline measured by centimeter is longer
than the same coastline measured by meter. How can this be?
Well, the centimeter can measure more of the coastline detail

than can a meter. So when the meter measurement is converted to centimeters, the measurement made by the centimeter is longer. Same coastline, different numbers, but both are correct, within their own context. In understanding a theory of how the world works, it is important to keep the context in which the theory is operating clearly in mind.

Historical alchemists were trying to resolve the question of how our universe operates through a variety of world-views, from Islamic mysticism to the supremacy of reason in Enlightenment Europe. Alchemists/philosophers, in their contemplation of the world of form, looked to the idea of elements—basic units from which the rest of the world was composed and built. Understanding what these elements are, how they behave, and how they can be manipulated, shifted, rotated, and changed, has been the driving force behind much of alchemy through the ages. These questions are still the basis of much of what we see in contemporary physics. It is all a question of framework and resolution and the questions we ask. As Werner Heisenberg, one of the developers of quantum theory, noted: "What we observe is not nature in itself but nature exposed to our method of questioning."[2]

The Elements

Aristotle (384–322 B.C.), in his *Metaphysics,* Book V, defined an element as "that out of which a thing is primarily composed, which is immanent in the thing and which is indivisible according to form." He initially held that there were four elements: Fire, Air, Water, and Earth. Plato (427–347 B.C.) in reference to the fifth geometric solid, the dodecahedron, ". . . the god used for arranging the constellations on the whole heaven,"[3] suggested a fifth element. Aristotle also elaborated upon a fifth element—*aither,* (*aether* in Latin). In English it is "ether," or "quintessence," and represents space. Most commonly, even the five elements are referred to in discussions as the Four Elements.

It was not only the Greeks who used this idea of four or five elements. As early as 1500 B.C. we see the idea of four elements in India. We also see the five elements in India, Tibet, and China, but with some variations. In India and Tibet there are fire, air, earth, water, and space. In China there are wood, fire, earth, metal, and water. In some philosophies in the East, the concept of space is seen as a "material" thing, a particle like the other four, as indicated in the *Kalachakra* tantra. In Western thought, Aristotle conceives of space as more a *place* in which something can occur.

Aristotle's Four Element theory was dominant throughout most of the history of alchemy. His *On the Heavens, Metaphysics, Physics,* and *On Generation and Corruption* and the thirteenth-century explication of these works by scholastics such as St. Thomas Aquinas were particularly important in forging the views of the philosophers.[4]

Aristotle and the scholastics were eventually put aside in a favor of a philosophy that looked to direct experience for answers rather than the statements of ancient authorities and their commentators.

An expression of this movement can be seen in the sixteenth century with the shift away from the Four Elements theory to one developed by the Swiss-German alchemist Philippus Aureolus Theophrastus Bombastus von Hohenheim, more commonly known as Paracelsus, who placed greater emphasis on what he termed the *Three Principles,* rather than the Aristotelian elements.

However, let us start at the beginning with the Great Elements, since this was the underlying dominant framework and mindset within which the alchemists, physicians, and philosophers all operated from 500 B.C.–1700 A.D. The following are definitions and associations of the Four Elements drawn from classical sources.

FIRE (First posited by Heraclitus). Empedocles—Hades (Typhon). Red. Feeling.

Aquinas defines Fire as a simple, that is, indivisible, body. It is hot and dry.

Avicenna (Ibn Sina). Its natural position is above all the other elements and is located in the region of the sublunary world—all that is beneath the Moon, in other words, our world.

It matures, rarefies, refines, and intermingles with all things. Its penetrative power enables it to traverse Air; with this power it subsumes the two heavy cold elements; by this power it keeps the elementary properties in harmony.[5]

It is that which expands, rises, and moves toward limits.

Any substance that is highly reactive or catalytic in nature is predominantly fire.

The Platonic solid is the tetrahedron.

AIR (First posited by Anaximenes). Empedocles—Zeus (Osiris). Yellow. Thinking.

Aquinas defines Air as a simple body. It is wet and hot.

Avicenna (Ibn Sina). Air lies above Water and beneath Fire. It rarefies, renders things finer, lighter, more delicate, softer, and consequently better able to move to a higher sphere.[6]

It is that which stretches and contracts, expands and rises, moving toward the limits.

Any substance that is a gas under normal conditions is predominantly Air.

The Platonic solid is the octahedron.

WATER (First posited by Thales). Empedocles—Persephone (Nephthys). Blue. Intuition.

Aquinas defines Water as a simple body. It is cold and wet.

Avicenna (Ibn Sina). Water surrounds Earth and is surrounded by Air. It allows things to be molded and spread out and attempered in their construction; it easily parts with an old shape and readily accepts a new one.[7]

It is that which contracts and falls.

It forms more toward the center.

Anything liquid is predominantly Water.

The Platonic solid is the icosahedron.

EARTH (First posited by Xenophanes). Empedocles—Hera (Isis). Green. Solidity, Persistence.

Aquinas defines Earth as a simple body. It is dry and cold.

Avicenna (Ibn Sina). Earth is the center of existence. It is stationary but returns to position if it is moved. It is by means of Earth that the parts of our body are fixed and held together into a compact form. This is how outward form is maintained.[8]

It is that which contracts and falls.

It forms more toward the center.

Anything solid under normal conditions is predominantly Earth.

The Platonic solid is the cube.

QUINTESSENCE, also called **the Ether.** This is the fifth element. It has no qualities and is the field, that is the source, of all matter and the space in which it exists.

The Platonic solid is the dodecahedron, the sphere of the twelve pentagons.

The Two Qualities

Aristotle described the formation of the Four Elements as the interplay between two qualities—active and passive. He described the active as "hot-cold," which causes bodies to coalesce. The passive is "dry-moist" which causes bodies to dissolve. The interplay of these two binaries gives rise to the Four Elements. In this system Fire is hot and dry; Air is hot and wet; Water is cold and wet; and Earth is cold and dry.

The order of the elements is, from the center out,
Earth, Water, Air, Fire and Space.

Of the elemental qualities, two are found in each element. However, in each element, one quality is primary and one quality is secondary.

Fire: *Hot*—primary. This is the higher of the active qualities or principles.
Dry—secondary. All moisture is consumed by the heat.

Air: *Wet*—primary. This is the higher of the passive qualities.
Hot—secondary. This is due to its closeness to Fire.

Water: *Cold*—primary. This is the second of the active qualities.
Wet—secondary. This is due to its closeness to Air.

Earth: *Dry*—primary. It is as though it had not been resolved into humidity because of its great distance from Fire. It is most dense.
Cold—secondary. This is due to its closeness to Water.

Rotation of Elements

We can clearly see how the elements are interlinked through a sharing of one of the two qualities that make up the element. The rotation of the elements is the change of one into another. Changing one of the qualities causes the rotation. More poetically expressed by Heraclitus (sixth century B.C.), "Fire lives the death of earth, and air lives the death of fire, water lives the death of air, earth that of water." Take for example, actual water—cold and wet. If we add heat we change the cold to hot, thereby actually transforming Water into Air—hot and wet, from water to steam. This is the principle, according to Aristotle, that allows the elements in nature to change, and it is heat that drives the rotation of elements in nature.

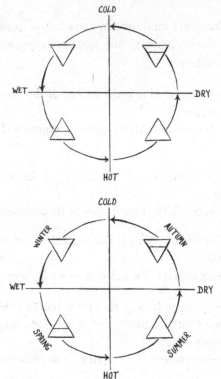

Aristotle: "It is clear that generation of the elements
will be circular." Earth to Water, Water to Air,
Air to Fire, Fire to Earth.

We make use of the rotation of the elements in the practice
of alchemy. We see Earth to Water in the melting of solids or
their dissolution in water; Water to Air in the boiling of water
or other solutions; Air to Water in distillation; Air to Fire in
combustion or calcinations and so on.

The Exhalations

In looking at concrete examples of metals and minerals, Aristotle[9] used the idea of two "exhalations"—that is, particular
formations of the Elements in transition—to explain their creation. There is a dry "earthy smoke" made of small particles of
Earth on their way to becoming Fire and a second wet "watery

vapor" made up of small particles of Water on their way to becoming Air. Stones, minerals, and metals are formed when the exhalations are trapped in the earth. When the dry "earthy smoke" dominates, stones and minerals are formed, and when the wet "watery vapor" dominates, metals are formed.

The Two Principles

The Sufi alchemist Jabir ibn Hayyan developed this theory further. He states that the two exhalations are not changed directly into metals or minerals but go through an intermediary stage. The "earthy smoke" is first converted into Sulphur and the "watery vapor" is converted into Mercury. It is the combination of Sulphur and Mercury in various proportions and purity, as well as the duration of gestation or coction in the earth, that gives rise to the varieties of metals and minerals. When they are pure and in equilibrium, gold is formed; when impure and imbalanced, lead, iron, copper, tin, silver, and so on are formed. We see here a theoretical basis for transmutation that can be put into practice. Since all metals are composed of the same materials, it is only a question of purifying and balancing the Sulphur and Mercury within the metal to transform it to its highest state, i.e., gold. The terms "Mercury" and "Sulphur" used here are to be considered in the abstract; they are not the actual element mercury (Hg) or the actual element sulphur (S).

But let's continue with the Mercury Sulphur theory as it became established in Europe. Here it is further explained by the Dominican scholar St. Albertus Magnus in his *Libellus de alchimia*:

> When pure red sulphur comes into contact with quicksilver in the earth, gold is made in a short or long time, either through the persistence (of the contact) or through decoction of the nature subservient to them. When pure and white sulphur comes into contact with quicksilver in pure earth, then silver is made, which differs from gold in this, that sulphur in gold will be

red, whereas in silver it will be white. When, on the other hand, red sulphur, corrupt and burning, comes into contact with quicksilver in the earth, then copper is made . . . When white sulphur, corrupt and burning, comes into contact with quicksilver in the earth, tin is made, . . . When white sulphur, corrupt and burning, comes into contact with quicksilver, in foetid earth, iron is made. When sulphur, black and corrupt, comes into contact with quicksilver, lead is made.[10]

From this we see the role that sulphur and mercury (quicksilver) play. Quicksilver is unchanging, regardless of what is formed, while the Sulphur tinges and gives form or character to the mix. We also see from this text the role that earth plays. Rather than being just a neutral matrix within which the Sulphur and Mercury can react, we see that the quality of the earth has a part to play in determining what metal will form. As you can see, we start with pure earth, go to earth, and then finally to foetid earth, and with each step, we move further from gold. This question of earth, or the body, or salt, was addressed here and there by individual alchemists, but it really wasn't "codified" into alchemical theory until the early sixteenth century by the Swiss-German physician and surgeon Paracelsus.

The Three Principles

Paracelsus added Salt to the two principles of Sulphur and Mercury to achieve the Three Principles, representing Body, Soul, and Spirit. This theory had a major impact on alchemy, with much of the subsequent work and writing of the alchemists speaking in terms of the Three Principles rather than the Four Elements.

MERCURY   SULPHUR   SALT
1: Spirit   *2: Soul*   *3: Body*

In Paracelsus' theory of Three Principles, Mercury signifies the quality of volatility, Sulphur signifies the quality of unctuousness, and Salt, the new addition, signifies solidity. Paracelsus defines the "Three prime Essences": Sulphur, he says, is whatever boils, an oil; Mercury is whatever rises as fumes, a liquor; and Salt is what remains in the ashes, an alkali. The terms indicate actual materials that make up a thing. Each thing can be broken down into its Mercury, Sulphur, and Salt, and this holds not just for the realm of metals and minerals but for all flora and fauna. As Paracelsus noted, "there are as many sulphurs, salts and mercuries as there are objects."[11] We will see this more specifically when we begin the actual work.

The Three Principles also resonated with Christian symbolism, primarily with the doctrine of the Holy Trinity. The two gnostic traditions of alchemy and Christian mysticism were used to interpret each other in light of the newest development in alchemical theory. For example, the Philosopher's Stone and the way to it are a metaphor for Christ and the way to Christ. We see this in the writings of Jacob Boehme and in the early Rosicrucian texts. So the theory of the Three Principles, bolstered inwardly and outwardly, gained ascendancy among the alchemists from Paracelsus onward and informs much of the alchemical practice.

All the above theories—the theory of elements; and of qualities; the theory of two principles or three principles—recognize that all come from one. The *Materia Prima*—The First Matter.

Materia Prima

The theory of *materia prima* and *forma substantia*—prime matter and substantial form, developed by Aristotle, states that it is from the interplay of prime matter and form that the elements, or principles, and subsequently, the whole of the material world, arise.

Materia prima is the "matter" that precedes actual substantial existence; it is formless "matter." It is pure potentiality of being. It is also called "hyle." *Forma substantia* is substantial form; it is that which gives existence to matter. Prime matter is pure potentiality and so it is dimensionless. It remains so until substantial form, also dimensionless, joins with it (prime matter); and from this union of the dimensionless rises the three dimensions and the beginnings of matter as we sense it. It then expands into three dimensions.

Aristotle believed prime matter and form, once joined, to be inseparable. But, like all theories, this changed and evolved as it was translated and commented upon by others—until we get to Paracelsus who asserted that "an object can be separated from its matter and continue to exist as a pure form which is transferable to matter." To take matter and reduce it to its prime matter is one of the steps necessary for transmutation. Alchemically speaking, prime matter is that state to which all can be reduced.

We also find, throughout the body of alchemical writings, a different use of the term *materia prima* or prime matter. At times it is used to mean the actual material that one begins to work upon. Be aware of which meaning is being used when confronted with it in an alchemical text.

To summarize: we see form and prime matter joined, giving rise to the Four Elements, each of which consists of two qualities, one from the active hot-cold pair, and one from the passive dry-moist pair. It is in the changing qualities that the elements are able to change into one another.

We can begin to see how alchemical theory shows a way into matter. The idea that there is a basic level of existence that, once understood, could be manipulated and transformed, guided the work of the alchemists. Their thinking was that in order to manipulate one layer of the physical world, one could go down a level to the underlying layer of organization and there effect a change. As the work was refined through practice and technique, and as the amount of energy needed to cause a separation and purification of the elements in question also increased, alchemists began to see things left over after the division of matter into the Four Elements.

The drive to better understand matter led to further conceptual divisions, and as the nature of matter became the central question, the attempt to further distinguish, refine, and categorize it continued, resulting in a plethora of elements. The process continues to this day. The latest count is well over 109 elements, counting the fleeting manifestations created in the physics laboratory. Below or within the elemental level lie the deeper worlds of atomic and subatomic particles. What began as two elements has become a menagerie. And where will it stop? Like two mirrors reflecting back upon themselves, it will not. Our perception simply recedes into darkness. The more light we pour in, the deeper we go and the more mirrors we can see. We are "digging" into "space," so to speak. It is a question of resolution.

Using our various levels of resolution, our theories, we can describe the world as being formed of Mercury, Sulphur, and Salt or of protons, neutrons, and electrons, or by any other system or schema. We can describe an atom of gold as being made up of seventy-nine protons, one hundred eighteen neutrons, and seventy-nine electrons, and lead as eighty-two protons, one hundred twenty-five neutrons, and eighty-two electrons. By losing three protons, seven neutrons, and three electrons, lead can theoretically be transmuted into gold. In 1919, Sir Ernest Rutherford showed through experiments with nitrogen that actual transmutation is possible. He was leery of the word "transmutation," fearing the ridicule of his fellow scientists, but by transforming nitrogen into oxygen, that is indeed what he accomplished. In the 1970s, in Darmstadt, Germany, the Society of Heavy Ion Research (GSI) used a heavy ion accelerator to successfully "punch out" proton-electron pairs from uranium. Matter that began with ninety-two protons and ninety-two electrons was eventually left with seventy-nine of each. Uranium had been effectively transmuted into gold.

I am not suggesting that this is what the alchemists were trying to do. Antoine-Joseph Pernety, in his definition of alchemy stated that true alchemy "employs the agency of Nature and imitates her operations" while false alchemy "works on erroneous principles and employs the tyrant and the destroyer of Nature for agency."[12] I am only suggesting that their framework was not that far removed from the framework of contemporary physics. It is a question of the energies involved as well as the detail of the theoretical framework used.

Gold, to the alchemists, was perfection. It is a metal that is incorruptible. Nothing corrodes it; nothing harms it, save *Aqua Regia,* the King's Water, a mix of hydrochloric acid and nitric acid. Gold, because of its perfection, rareness, and beauty, is highly valued. The metals were seen to be on a spectrum from impure and corruptible to pure and incorruptible—that is, from lead to gold. Some alchemists described gold as a perfect blend and balance of the Three Principles: pure Mercury, pure Sulphur, and pure Salt. Lead was seen as an overabundance of impure, raw Mercury, a little Sulphur, and a heavy yet porous Salt. Lead is thus an unripe immature gold. By finishing what nature had started by separating, purifying, and balancing the Three Principles and recombining them, lead could be completed and perfected, transmuted into gold. Indeed, any aspect of creation can be moved from imperfection to perfection; as Paracelsus stated, alchemy can "carry to its end something that has not yet been completed."

CHAPTER TWO

COSMOLOGY

It is important to understand these theories and to actually build up a visual image of the universe they depict. It is a universe in which all things are linked. What the theories enable us to do is to articulate and use some of the links. The first major link is expressed best by the phrase from *Tabula smaragdina,* The Emerald Tablet (see chapter six), "as above, so below." This link is the link between the macrocosmos, that is, the heavens, stars, Sun, Moon, and planets, and the microcosmos, that is, life here on Earth. This link shows that changes in the macrocosmos cause or reflect the changes in the microcosmos.

The architectural blueprint of the cosmos used in alchemy is the Ptolemaic system, a modified form of Aristotle's cosmology which places the earth in the center of the universe. The Four Elements—Earth, Water, Air, and Fire—tend to fall in order from the center out, and generally fit our experience of the physical world. Beyond these four is the Ether, which is divided into shells. Each shell revolves and carries a planet. In the past the planets weren't seen as orbiting balls of matter as we conceive of them today, but were seen by some as either a luminous spot on the otherwise transparent shell, or as a hole in the shell through which energy or "fire" from higher up, blasted through. There was no space between the transparent planetary shells, so as they moved they were thought to create a kind of music full of harmony and discord, described as the "music of the spheres" by Pythagoras (580–500 B.C.) and his followers.

Planetary Spheres

Working our way up from Earth, Water, Air, Fire, we come to the Sphere of the Moon—the first shell, the first division of the Ether, of the unchanging perfection, incorruptible as opposed to the world beneath the Moon, the sublunary realm, the world of change. The Sphere of the Moon is the boundary between this world of change and the realm of unchanging perfection, and so begins the ascent.

Ptolemaic universe
From Johannes Hevelius' Selenographia.

☽ The **Moon** is cold and moist, most of its power is humidifying, and it softens and causes putrefaction. What small amount of heat it does give comes from the Sun. Feminine. The Moon is associated with emotions, instincts, and motherhood. Subconscious. Memory. The Realm of Dreams. Passive. Changeable. Receives energy. In the body it rules the stomach, breasts, womb, bodily fluids, and the left side. Silver. Night. Monday. Zodiac: Fourth House. Cancer. Deities: Diana, Artemis, Selene, and Khons.

☿ **Mercury** is cold and dry when masculine, cold and moist when feminine, androgynous. It is drying and absorptive of moisture and at times humidifying, it quickly changes between the two. It takes on the quality of the sign it is in. Mind. Communication. Principle of Intellect. Body: arms, hands, shoulders, lungs, solar plexus, abdomen, intestines, nervous and respiratory systems. Quicksilver (mercury). Wednesday. Zodiac: Third and Sixth Houses, Gemini and Virgo. Deities: Mercury, Hermes, and Thoth.

♀ **Venus** is warm and moist, it warms moderately but mostly humidifies like the Moon. Feminine. Affection, love, beauty. Principle of Attraction. Body: neck, kidneys, ovaries, veins and their circulation. Copper. Friday. Zodiac: Second and Seventh Houses, Taurus and Libra. Deities: Venus, Aphrodite, and Isis.

☉ **The Sun** is hot and dry, its essential nature is heating and to a lesser degree, drying. Masculine. Vitality, ego, individuality. Principle of Fatherhood. Authority. Body: heart, back, spine and spinal cord, the right side. Gold. Sunday. Zodiac: Fifth House, Leo. Deities: Sol, Apollo, Helios, and Ra.

♂ **Mars** is hot and dry, its nature is to dry and to burn. Masculine. Energy and drive. Principle of Active Desire. Initiatory, aggressive. Body: head, muscles, sex organs, anus, virility, forcefulness. Iron. Tuesday. Zodiac: First and Eighth Houses, Aries and Scorpio. Deities: Mars, Ares, and Horus.

♃ **Jupiter** is warm and moist it heats and humidifies. It is a temperate active force, and "produces fertilizing winds." Masculine. Ethical, Moral values, Philosophy. Abstract mind. Principle of Expansion. Body: blood, arteries and circulation, hips, thighs, feet, liver. Ample, plentiful. Tin. Thursday. Zodiac: Ninth and Twelfth Houses, Sagittarius and Pisces. Deities: Jupiter, Zeus, and Ammoun.

♄ **Saturn** is cold and dry, its nature is to cool and moderately to dry. Masculine. Principle of Contraction and Restriction. Discipline, responsibility. Body: bones, joints, knees, spleen, skin and teeth. Discipline and restriction. Lead. Saturday. Zodiac: Tenth and Eleventh Houses, Capricorn and Aquarius. Deities: Saturn, Kronos, and Nephthys.

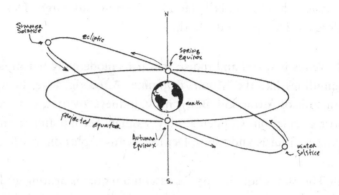

We come next to the Sphere of the Fixed Stars against which the planets move. The narrow band of sky that the Sun appears to travel through is called the ecliptic. The constellations along the ecliptic are called the signs of Zodiac, which begins with Aries and ends with Pisces. The spring equinox, the beginning of the astrological year, is called the first point of Aries and is defined as 0° Aries. This holds true regardless of the actual astronomical constellation now at the first point of Aries.[13]

The spring equinox is the center of practice. It is a seasonal relationship that determines the positions of the Zodiacal signs in the heavens, not the position of the fixed stars that make up those constellations astronomically. From here we can observe a framework that can describe time, space, and Earth in terms of the Four Elements as well as the Zodiac and the seasons. By understanding the concepts and definitions of the Four Elements, their two qualities, and most important, *materia prima* and *forma substantia*, we can see how this system informs all areas of exploration: astronomy, astrology, and medicine. This elemental interlinking of the outer world with the inner world makes for a very powerful and potent mandala.

Later philosophers, mystics, and theologians divided the Ether beyond the Sphere of the Fixed Stars even further. They created or expressed a realm of Intelligences and Angels before arriving at the source of creation's emanation—God. They did this to reconcile the Aristotelian Ptolemaic view, that matches up very well with the observable world and sky, and with the Bible, particularly Genesis.

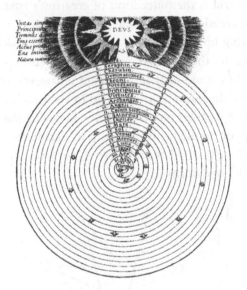

Robert Fludd. Tomus Secundus de Supernaturali . . . *1619.*

Begin to build up and visualize an image of the cosmos with the elemental links and planetary interconnections. Imagine this sphere from the outside looking in. Through the fixed stars, through the transparent spheres of Saturn, Jupiter, Mars, the Sun, Venus, Mercury, the Moon, and in the center of the sphere is our world, the world of the Four Elements, the world of ceaseless change and turmoil. Imagine this luminous sphere suspended in what St. Dionysus the Areopagite described as "the brilliant darkness of a hidden silence."[14]

This is essentially a map of how the energy of creation moves from impulse to its ultimate end in the world of matter. What God does at creation, the alchemist attempts to replicate in the laboratory. The energy of the cosmos flows from the Creator through the planets to the sublunary world, each sphere transmitting as well as adding its own imprint as the impulse moves from beyond the fixed stars toward manifestation. All parts have a role to play in creation, and each created thing bears the stamp of the forces at play in its particular birth. The material world is the outer limit of creation's emanation; it is the end of creation, from subtle to gross.

Knowing how the cosmos is structured allows us to work "according to the celestial opportunity," that is, when the planetary forces are at their optimum. However, work can be done at any time, just as you can go to the beach anytime you care to go. A weather report, however, knowing the disposition of the play of the elements, will help to decide the best time to go to the beach, whether it's to swim, surf, or photograph the incoming winter storm.

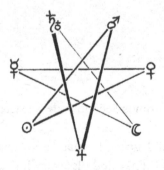

The flow of energy from Saturn to Earth.

CHAPTER THREE

TIME

Whosoever will work according to the celestial opportunity,
ought to observe both or one of them, namely the
motion of the stars, or their times . . .[1]

—HENRY CORNELIEUS AGRIPPA OF NETTESHEIM

In the creative process, knowing when to do something is just
as important as knowing how to do it. Things arise, unfold,
and decay—interacting throughout. We must learn how to
ride the currents. What follow are some charts and diagrams
of how this all connects, how energy ebbs and flows in this
pulsing, evolving, ever-changing cosmos.

Solar Year

The year is a solar cycle and can be divided by two, three, four,
and twelve.

DIVISION BY TWO

The year can be halved using two different methods. One
method follows the natural cycle of the outgoing phase and
the ingoing phase we see in the life cycle of plants. The outgoing phase, from Aries through Virgo, the beginning of spring
to the end of summer, is the period in which plants sprout,
flower, fruit, and go to seed. Mythologically, this is the time
during which Pluto allowed his wife Persephone, to visit the
earth's surface as part of the marriage arrangement. The ingoing phase, from Libra through Pisces, the beginning of fall to
the end of winter, the time when Persephone returned to the
underworld to be with Pluto, is the period in which plants go
dormant or die entirely.

The other way of dividing the year in two is by way of the Sun and the Moon. The first half, the Solar half, starts with a Fire sign, Leo, and ends with an Earth sign, Capricorn. Following what was established earlier regarding the rotation of the elements and the two qualities of warm-cold and dry-wet, we see that by starting with Fire and ending with Earth we essentially have a dry path, in that Fire dries and separates the other elements. The second half, the Lunar half, starts with an Air sign, Aquarius, and ends with a Water sign, Cancer, and shows us essentially a wet way. We can use these cycles to harmonize timings with the work at hand. Processes that have as a result a solid, condensed material should be worked on within the dry half of the cycle. And likewise, those that have a liquid result should be done within the wet half.

The division of the solar year.

DIVISION BY THREE

The first period, from Aries to Cancer (spring to the first month of summer), a time of lengthening days, is one of rebirth, growth, flowering, and ripening. The second period, from Leo through Scorpio (the last months of summer through the first month of fall), a time of shortening daylight, is one of fruition and harvest. The third period, from Sagittarius through Pisces (last months of autumn through the end of winter), a time of the shortest days and longest nights, is one of seeming death, as the forces of the Earth that nourished the year draw inward. The Earth, as it lies dormant, gathers its regenerative power into the roots and seeds.

These three phases—arising, enduring, decaying—can be associated with the Three Principles of Mercury, Sulphur, and Salt, respectively.

DIVISION BY FOUR

Dividing the year by the Four Elements gives us the four seasons, each an expression of one of the Elements. The year starts with spring. Exceeding in moisture, spring is the expression of the element of Air—wet and warm. From Aries to Gemini we feel the initial burst of solar energy that will course its way through the Zodiac. It is a time of the first stirrings of life to its flower. Summer, exceeding in heat, follows. It is Fire— warm and dry. What flowered in spring comes to fruition from Cancer to Virgo. As the heat of summer leads to dryness, we come to autumn that exceeds in dryness. It is the season of the element Earth—dry and cold. As the Sun moves through Libra to Sagittarius, the plants in their fruition go to seed. From Capricorn to Pisces, the year comes to end with Water—cold and wet. Winter exceeds in cold, the energy that began the year withdraws, seeds become dormant, and roots gather energy for the coming year.

DIVISION BY TWELVE

The division by twelve begins at the first point of Aries and gives us the twelve traditional signs of the zodiac.

♈ Aries—Mars, beginnings. Cardinal, Fire, Positive, Action, Most associations shared with Mars.

♉ Taurus—Venus, determined effort. Fixed, Earth, Negative, endurance, Most associations shared with Venus.

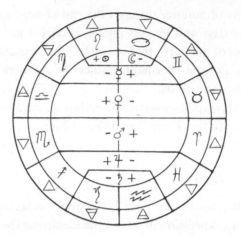

The zodiac with its planetary and elemental attributions.

♊ **Gemini**—Mercury, diversified action, intellectual drive. Air, Positive, Most associations shared with Mercury.

♋ **Cancer**—Moon, emotional drive, changeable. Water, Negative, Most associations shared with the Moon.

♌ **Leo**—Sun, authoritative action, noble effort. Fire, Positive, Most associations shared with the Sun.

♍ **Virgo**—Mercury, methodical action, discriminating. Earth, Negative, Most associations shared with Mercury.

♎ **Libra**—Venus, cooperative action, harmony. Air, Positive, Most associations shared with Venus.

♏ **Scorpio**—Mars, intense action, passionate drive. Water, Negative, Most associations shared with Mars.

♐ **Sagittarius**—Jupiter, zealous action, idealistic drive. Fire, Positive, Most associations shared with Jupiter.

♑ **Capricorn**—Saturn, organized action, status-seeking drive. Earth, Negative, Most associations shared with Saturn.

≈ **Aquarius**—Saturn, progressive action, altruistic drive. Air, Positive, Most associations shared with Saturn.

⯓ **Pisces**—Jupiter, subdued action, lethargic drive. Water, Negative, Most associations shared with Jupiter.

A planet rules each of these signs, and, depending on the position within the zodiac of a particular planet, the planet's function is either enhanced or diminished. If the planet is in a sign friendly to it, such as the Sun is to Leo, its function and power is enhanced. Conversely, if the planet is found in a sign unfriendly to it, such as the Moon in Leo, its function and power is diminished. The full relationships between planets and signs may be found in any book on astrology.

Lunar Month

The Moon is a factor in alchemical work, particularly in working with plants, due to the Moon's rule over the Plant Kingdom. The work should ideally follow and move with the phases of the Moon. The lunar cycle may be divided by two, by four, by seven, by twelve, and by twenty-eight, as well as into a diurnal cycle related to the tides.

The first division is one that takes the full lunation cycle and separates it into two—a waxing period and a waning period. The waxing is just that, the increase of the Moon's light from new Moon to full Moon, and is a period generally of growth, increase, and any other positive, constructive sense we may wish to bring to this notion. The waning is the decrease of the Moon's light from full Moon to new Moon. This period is one of decay, separation, and any other negative, destructive sense we may give to this idea. This cycle can be visualized as the life cycle of a plant.

In fact, to work with the Moon, one should first conceive of an action or process in terms of a plant's life cycle—of its qualities as the plant goes from seed, to sprout, to bloom, to fruit, to seeds—and then relate each to the phases of the Moon.

When you can understand what part or aspect of the process represents what part or aspect of the life cycle, you can then harmonize your work with the Moon as it moves from New Moon seed to Full Moon bloom to seed again.

The Full Moon strengthens the alchemical technique.

New Moon to First Quarter is productive of moisture. It represents the seed to sprout, the inception of an action and its initial growth.

First Quarter to Full Moon is productive of heat. It represents the sprout to the bloom.

Full Moon to Last Quarter is productive of dryness. It represents the bloom to its fruit. The completion and realization of the New Moon: the quality of the New Moon becomes concrete at the full Moon. It is the beginning of the crystallization and later disintegration.

Last Quarter to New Moon is productive of cold. It represents the fruit to the seeds. The action is now completed. Dormancy or decomposition begins along with the dissemination of the seeds.

The alchemical processes, symbolized by the Signs of the Zodiac, are strengthened by the presence of the Full Moon in the respective sign. Sublimation, for example, is boosted by the presence of the Full Moon in Libra.

In general, the completion of the work should coincide with the Moon's return to the Sun. The key point is when the Moon is one minute from the Sun. This has been compared to the joy a returning traveler feels as she approaches the very door to her home.

Planetary Days and Hours

Planetary time is the time—that is, the day and the hours—distributed to the planets' dominions. The Lunar Month is divided by the Four Elements, giving a cycle of seven days. Each day of the cycle is ruled by one of the seven planets. The Sun rules Sunday; The Moon, Monday; Mars, Tuesday; Mercury, Wednesday; Jupiter, Thursday; Venus, Friday; and Saturn, Saturday.

The day itself is divided into hours, and each hour has a planetary ruler. The day is first divided into two, day and night, each of twelve hours following the custom of the Romans. There are several schemes for doing this, each based on a different interpretation of the start of the day and the length of the hours. The system that was most used in the fifteenth and sixteenth centuries was recorded by Cornelius Agrippa (1486–1535), and it holds that the planet that rules the day rules the first hour of the day. The next hour is ruled by the next planet according to the following order: Sun, Venus, Mercury, Moon, Saturn, Jupiter, and Mars.

The first hour of the day is the hour of sunrise; the hour of sunset is the first hour of night. Night and day are divided evenly by twelve, giving unequal "hours." So an "hour" of daylight during summer would be longer than sixty minutes and an "hour" of daylight during winter could be as short as forty-five minutes.

Below (Figure 1) is the system diagrammed as a spiral, with 6:00 a.m. given as the hour of sunrise at the equinox for convenience.

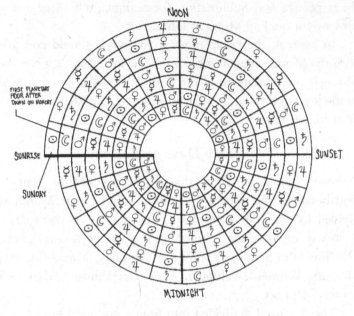

Figure 1

All of this would be used to determine the best time to do something. For instance, if one was to work with iron one might, in order to harmonize the action better with the cosmos, time the key parts of the work to occur when Mars is well aspected or rules the hour for the work at hand.

Most important, however, is to work with a sense of harmony and not slavishly follow the rules. Understand the work that is being done. Get inside of it and create a unified work of the inner and outer elements. Poetry involves the following of the rules, but the best poets play with the rules to create surprising juxtapositions and beauty, not only in form and content but also in the ultimate meanings. Alchemy brings this sense of a living art to all its operations.

CHAPTER FOUR

Microcosm:
The Body and Its Composition

W̶e now have the roughest outline of the cosmos and some
of the major links. Now let us examine the human—the
microcosm, the reflection of all that is above.

The body is a dynamic blend of elements as well as its own
celestial system, which can be expressed in terms of the Sun,
Moon, planets, and stars. The Four Elements are expressed in
the body as humors: Fire—Blood, Air—Yellow Bile, Water—
Phlegm, and Earth—Black Bile. Each humor has a function in
and of itself, in addition to keeping the other humors in balance.

The four humors in turn give rise to the four tempera-
ments: Blood—Sanguine, Yellow Bile—Choleric, Phlegm—
Phlegmatic, and Black Bile—Melancholic. Like the Elements,
they are all present, but usually it is one or two of the temper-
aments that dominate the picture and express themselves more
strongly and clearly, showing in the appearance, character, and
manner of the individual. The Sanguine individual is typically
happy, optimistic, passionate, proud, and fiery. The Choleric
is more practical and rational, impatient, angry, and irrita-
ble. The Phlegmatic reflects the qualities of water, sensitive,
peaceful, soft, brooding, and sad. The Melancholic is generally
intelligent, cultured, restless, and depressive.

It is the particular individual's balance of the elements/
humors that determines the health of that individual. Much of
early European medicine is based on the four humors, with the
healing process focused on returning the humors to their former balance through a variety of therapeutic techniques, such
as drugs, purgations, and bleeding.

Since the body is a microcosm, we find the planets and the stars represented there too. We see that a planetary rulership is ascribed to various organs, and there is a zodiacal correspondence to the body also.

The point of all this is to show how this interlocking worldview is the framework of the practice. All these pieces come out of the arrangement and expression of the elements in time and space. Take time to work out a diagram of your own, which you will build upon and modify as you develop it. Use this diagram as the basis of visualization. Learn it so well you can actually see it. See it so well you can actually move about in it.

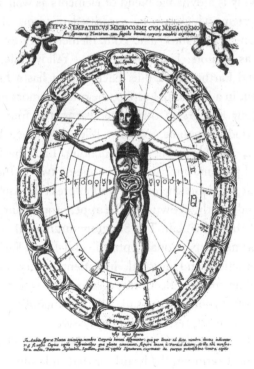

The intersection of Heaven and Earth is reflected in the celestial anatomy of the human body. From Athanasius Kircher's Oedipus Aegyptiacus, *1653.*

The Greeks developed a system of memory for oratory. It entails visualizing a building and associating the different rooms and contents with different parts of the speech. The more unusual the object in the room, the stronger is the memory link. So when the time came to deliver the speech, the orator would imagine walking through the building and picking up the segments of the oratory. In this way it was possible to recite very long speeches.

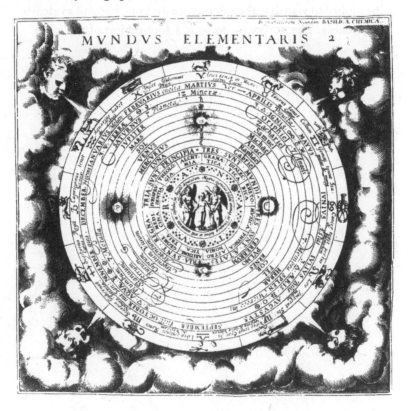

From Museum Hermeticum Reformatum et Amplificatum, *1678.*

Giordano Bruno, Raymond Lull, and others developed this further with a more hermetic intent. They developed systems that are truly mandala-building in that they integrate all aspects of existence into one encompassing blueprint to be used as a tool for gnosis.

These systems are very similar to many of the Buddhist mandalas, if not in the specific details of their architecture, certainly in the overall sense of interlocking associations of both micro- and macrocosmic phenomena and, perhaps, shared intent. These blueprints, these mandalas, are memorized and visualized in three dimensions. It is highly desirable to develop the ability to visualize the microcosm and macrocosm as clearly as possible. The ability to do so is a foundation of the work.

CHAPTER FIVE

INNER PRACTICE

☿

When you make the two one, and when you make the inside
like the outside and the outside like the inside, and the above
like the below, and when you make the male and the female
one and the same . . . then you will enter the Kingdom.[1]

—THE GOSPEL OF THOMAS

Alchemy is a technique or path of gnosis. Gnosis, which comes from the Greek gnosis meaning "knowledge," is a belief in just that—direct knowledge of God. In general, gnostic faiths hold that the soul is trapped in matter, imperfect, and impure, but that through certain practices one can free oneself from the habitual prison of matter and achieve a *unio mystica*, a "mystical union" with God. In the first few centuries of our era, many of the religions and philosophies were gnostic in their intent. They varied widely, however, in their dogmas, cosmology, origins, views on the material world and body, ritual, and the path and stages to union with God. There were Jewish gnostics, Christian gnostics, Manicheans, hermeticists, the actual Gnostic religion, and later Moslem gnostics, all of whom had a hand in forming alchemy. The alchemical view holds that essence is trapped in matter, our inner light imprisoned by matter or obscured by our material fog. Alchemy shows a way of ascent, the return to God. It is through matter itself that we may find our way. It is an approach to the divine through matter.

Alchemy can be aligned with each tradition and its mystical practices. To properly do the inner work with alchemy, it is highly advisable to work within a particular tradition. It is also good to examine the other traditions, as doing so can help to inform your own. But keep your actual practices to one tradition and work there.

One can use alchemy as a *ladder of ascent* by finding the symbolism within the materials and processes and working *without as within* using the materials and processes as a support for the inner work. This may seem like nothing until you feel the movements and shifts in the material in the creative process.

Alchemy holds that matter, the body, is not in itself bad and can actually be used as an aid in the *unio mystica,* the *Opus Magnum* or Great Work. The material world is appropriated toward an inner, more spiritual world. So to this end the material world or the human body is not denied, tortured, or abused. It is kept strong and healthy.

This is also a role of alchemy—the creation of medicines to keep the body healthy and to preserve life. The point is not to amass more gold, more things, but to have more time and energy to pursue the inner work and to benefit others.

There is one thing necessary for inner work, or for any work: a steady mind. It is of the utmost importance that the mind be strong, supple, and focused; that it is able to stay where you place it, and isn't knocked about by the incessant chatter and noise of your thoughts. Without a steady mind, no real progress can be made. Developing this then becomes the first and foremost step in the practice of alchemy. Here is a very simple and basic technique of using the breath as a focus of contemplation. This technique is not actually contemplation or meditation but is rather the mechanics of the technique. It is a good exercise in and of itself or as a warm-up to actual meditation.

To begin, we breathe normally and just allow the attention to follow the breath out and then in, not forcing the breath, just allowing it to happen. We then begin to count breathing cycles, starting on the out breath. It is: exhale, inhale—one; exhale, inhale—two; and so on up to ten. When you notice you are no longer counting the breaths, start over. Continue doing this for about three or five minutes at first. You will find at the beginning that it is very difficult to even complete one cycle of ten without your mind being carried off by some random mental chatter. But with persistence and a consistent practice you will be able to focus more sharply and clearly. As you get accustomed to the practice, try extending it in length. After a point, you will be able to follow the breath through several rounds and, after great practice, for as long as you like. With consistent practice it does get easier. And with that ease you can begin to see what a powerful tool the mind is. That is where the fun begins.

I would like to note here that this practice will get you started and get you quite far, but as you progress, you may want to go further and get past some inevitable roadblocks. To this end, find yourself a very qualified meditation instructor.

In actual meditation the only thing that changes is the object of meditation. It can be a visualization or an analysis of an object's composition, a recitation, or a review of a process. The technique of holding the mind to the object remains the same.

Throughout the discussion of theory there have been suggestions to visualize some of the cosmological relationships as well as the overall cosmological blueprint or mandala. To visualize something is, ideally, to see it in your mind's eye as clearly as you see the world. That ideal is something to work toward. It is a learnable skill that develops, like any other skill, with steady practice. We all know how to visualize. We do it every day. Here is a very simple exercise: Imagine in your mind's eye that you get up from where you are and walk out onto the nearest walkway. Now describe what you see there. Some of it may be from memory that lists the places you would pass, some of it will be a visual sense, a sense of seeing, rather than listing. Put your attention to the visual sense. Start walking and keep describing what you see or remember. Do this frequently; take walks in your imagination of real routes that you take. In time, you will discover that you can actually see the entire walk in your mind's eye. You can do this with anything, such as the surface of your desk or dresser. Try to mentally picture it, and name what you see on the desk or dresser. This same process is done with symbols, images, and cosmological diagrams.

With complex images it is best to start with the broadest outlines and then bring into focus and fill in the details, generally working from the center out or from the most symbolically significant. Keep a consistent practice, and in time you will be able to visualize as clearly as you see the world. This is yet another powerful tool.

With these powerful tools and knowledge of the materials and processes that follow, there is great potential for either good things or bad things to happen. Alchemists warn about certain knowledge in the hands of evil, greedy people and the harm it can bring—and so urge secrecy and discretion. This is important to both protect the work and as a means of keeping the noise down, since much of the alchemical work must be done undisturbed. So silence becomes yet another key. In fact, one should strive to remove or at least reduce all sources of conflict and disruption around the work in particular and in one's life in general, reducing further the level of noise. Create only good, and only good will come.

It is also part of the tradition that, with one's success with the *Opus Magnum,* the "Great Work," one should care for the poor and sick. The legendary French alchemist Nicholas Flamel and his *soror mystica,* ("mystical sister,") Perenelle, succeeded in the Great Work, not just once, but three times, and on April 25, 1382, at five o'clock in the evening, transmuted a half a pound of mercury into pure gold of the highest quality. Flamel notes in his *Exposition of the Hieroglyphical Figures* that by the year 1413 they had "already founded, and endued with revenues, 14 Hospitals in this City of Paris, we had now built from the ground three Chapels. . . I will not speak of the good which both of us have done to particular poor folks, principally to widows and poor orphans."[2]

The beginning of all alchemical action should be dedicated to the alleviation of suffering, and any results should be given over to the alleviation of suffering.

Alchemy is the union of the Sun and the Moon. From Theatrum Chemicum Britannicum, *1652.*

CHAPTER SIX

TABULA SMARAGDINA

The *Tabula smaragdina* ("The Emerald Tablet") is the very heart of alchemy. It is considered to be one of the oldest alchemical texts. Legend has it that it was found near Hebron in a cave that was the tomb of Hermes, called Thoth by the Egyptians. Hermes/Thoth is the god of writing, science, and math. Depending on the version, the tomb was discovered by Zara (Sarah) wife of Abraham, Alexander the Great, or Apollonius of Tyanna. The Emerald Tablet is just that, a tablet of emer-ald upon which, engraved in Phoenician, is a teaching on alchemy by Hermes. After its discovery it is thought to have made its way from the Greeks into Islam via Syria. An Arabic version appears in Jabir ibn Hayyan's *Second Book of the Elements of the Foundation,* and another Arabic version is to be found in *The Secret of Creation* by Apollonius (813–887 A.D.), which places the earliest documented text around 800 A.D., although

Tabula smaragdina

it is believed that the text is based on an earlier Greek document. From Islam the *Tabula smaragdina* entered Europe in the twelfth century, translated from Arabic into Latin by Hugo of Satalla in Tarazona. Mention of it is made by Albertus Magnus in his *De rebus metallicis et mineralibus*. There were various translations and versions of the Emerald Tablet, but it was the one printed in 1541 that became the most widely known. That is the one I reproduce here. I also include the emblem that has been traditionally associated with the Emerald Tablet since 1588, and that was joined to the text to elucidate or depict the teaching engraved on the *Tabula smaragdina*.

The *Tabula smaragdina* is one of the roots of alchemy. Read it, study it, track down its various sources, read it again, then meditate on it. Memorize it, and you will always have it with you to refer to as the work progresses. At the very least, a copy of the *Tabula smaragdina* should be tacked above your workbench and read and contemplated before working. Meditate on it, line by line, word by word, and it will gradually open itself to you as you gain understanding from the actual work.

Tabula Smaragdina

Verum, sine mendacio, certum et verissimum:
Quod est inferius est sicut quod est superius. Et quod
est superius est sicut quod est inferius, ad perpe-
tranda miracula rei unius. Et sicut res omnes fuer-
unt ab uno, meditatione unius. Sic omnes res natae
fuerunt ab hac una re, adaptatione.
Pater eius est Sol, mater eius Luna. Portavit illud ven-
tus in ventre suo. Nutrix eius terra est. Pater omnis
telesmi totius mundi est hic. Vis eius integra est, si
versa fuerit in terram. Separabis terram ab igne,
subtile ab spisso, suaviter, cum magno ingenio.
Ascendit ab terra in coelum, iterumque descendit in
terram, et recipit vim superiorum et inferiorum.
Sic habebis gloriam totius mundi. Ideo fugiet ab te
omnis obscuritas. Hic est totius fortitudinis forti-

tudo fortis, quia vincet omnem rem subtilem, omne-
mque solidam penetrabit.
Sic mundus creatus est. Hinc erunt adaptationes mira-
biles, quarum modus hic est. Itaque vocatus sum
Hermes Tris-megistus, habens tres partes philoso-
phiae totius mundi.
Completum est quod dixi de operatione Solis.

The Emerald Tablet

True, without lie, certain and most true.

That which is below is as that which is above, and that
which is above is as that which is below, to accomplish the miracles of the One.

And as all things came from the One by the contemplation of the One, thus all things arise from this one
thing by adaptation.

Its father is the Sun, its mother is the Moon. The wind
carried it in its belly. Its nurse is the earth.

The Father of every miracle in the whole world is here.

Its power is complete, if it will be turned into[1] earth.

You shall separate earth from fire, the subtle from the
gross, gently and with great ingenuity.[2]

It ascends from earth to heaven, and again descends
into the earth, and receives the powers of the things
above and below. Thus you shall have the glory of
the whole world. All obscurity shall fly from you.

This is the strength of every strength, for it overcomes
every subtle thing and shall penetrate every solid
thing.

Thus the world was created.

From this shall come marvelous adaptations, of which
this is the method.

Therefore I am called Hermes Trismegistus, having the
three parts of the philosophy of the whole world.

It is completed that which I had to say about the operation of the Sun.

Part Two

PRACTICE

CHAPTER SEVEN

THE BASICS OF ALCHEMY

*Nature must serve as the basis and model of science, and Art
must work according to Nature as far as possible, therefore,
the Artist must observe Nature and
operate how she operates.*[1]

—St. Albertus Magnus

Here we enter into the body of alchemy—the physical process. Nature must lead both in material and in method. Nature is your true book. Study it well.

Take the time to look around, really. Refamiliarize yourself with the matter of the world, the space of the world, and the movement of the world. Find the materials you wish to work with. Get samples of the minerals and metals and begin to study them directly. Start with the raw materials as close to the source as possible. All raw materials should be considered as living and should be processed and worked with clear intent. Think of the difference between a meal prepared with fresh ingredients in season as opposed to one prepared with frozen or stale components.

One can of course use the chemical equivalents of the raw materials: diluted acetic acid as opposed to distilled red wine vinegar, for example, but recognize that this is not alchemy. It can, however, be used to practice and study the *techniques* of alchemy without wasting some very precious material. It is somewhat like a doing a small color study for a larger painting and saving the lapis lazuli and gold for the painting. The best advice is to get into the habit of preparing all materials from as close to the source as possible.[2] Just preparing the raw materials will teach you much in the way of technique.

Atalanta fugiens. *Emblem 42. Michael Maier, 1604.*

Jabir ibn Hayyan identified four basic techniques necessary for the practice of alchemy: *purification, solution, coagulation,* and *combination.* Purification involves the separation of the impure from the pure and is done either by fire—calcinations or sublimation; or by water—distillation or filtration. Solution is accomplished through maceration and dissolution. Coagulation can be done by crystallization, congelation, or evaporation. Combination is achieved by circulation, cohobation, digestion, crystallization, or fixation. To be more specific:

Calcination is the burning of anything to ashes. It is the burning off of all combustible impurities. It can mean to melt a metal in the presence of air while stirring it, oxidizing the metal and forming a calx.

Circulation is the gentle heating of a solution and a cooling of its vapors. The condensation flows back into the original solution. The solution rotates from liquid to vapor to liquid continuously.

Cohobation is the taking of a distillate and pouring it back over what-ever remains of the material from which it was distilled.

Congelation is the turning of a liquid into a solid, as in water congealing to solid ice. It can also mean a solidification of a mass due the loss of water or other solvent. It can mean crystallization.

Crystallization is the opening of a body or the congealing of a liquid around solid matter. It forms a beautiful matrix in which the salt is suspended. Most salts when dissolved in water, and the water evaporated, will form crystals. It is also used to purify salt.

Digestion is a slow, gentle "cooking." It helps break down some things so that they will have a better, more intimate mix with other things. Generally the mixture is placed in a flask and sealed. This flask is then put in a warm and dark place and kept at around 40°C.

Dissolution is just that, the dissolving of one substance, the solute, into a liquid, the solvent.

Distillation is the extraction of a liquor from a body or solution by heating and then cooling, condensing the vapor, and collecting the resulting liquid, the distillate.

Evaporation is the removal of the more volatile portions of a mixture by exposing it to the atmosphere and, at times, by gently heating the mixture to accelerate the process.

Fermentation is the breaking down of the plant and the release of its Mercury that is alcohol, with the aid of a ferment or yeast. A similar process occurs in the mineral kingdom.

Filtration is a mechanical means of separating particulate matter from a liquid. It is generally accomplished through the use of filter papers, fritted glass, screens, and funnels.

Fixation is to make that which is volatile nonvolatile. How this is accomplished varies from material to material.

Maceration is actually a form of dissolution. Typically it refers to the soaking of herbs in a solution of water or alcohol. It takes about two to three days to allow a proper maceration in water. If the time is too short not all the virtues are put into solution. If left too long, decomposition and fermentation may start. When macerating with alcohol solutions, there is no real time limit.

Multiplication is a process in the Great Work where the strength of the Philosopher's Stone is augmented.

Projection is a process in the Great Work where the Philosopher's Stone is tested by changing lead or mercury into gold or silver.

Putrefaction is the decomposition of the impurities of the body, the ephemeral parts. It is a form of purification, all in preparation for the opening of the body.

Sublimation is the purification of certain salts or minerals that exhibit the ability, when heated sufficiently, to change from solid to gas and back to solid without going through the liquid phase. Sal ammoniac is a good and useful example of a salt that is purified in this manner.

These are the techniques used in the manipulation of matter, in the rotation of the elements. And, as you may remember, it is heat that drives the rotation of the elements both in nature and in art, making the management of fire extremely important. Alchemical practice recognizes Four Degrees of Fire:

The **First Degree** is a soft and gentle heat accomplished through a *Balneum vaporis*, a steam bath in which the flask is heated by suspending it over the steam of boiling water.

It can also be done with a *Balneum marie*, Maria's Bath,[3] (See Figure 2 on page 51) that is a water bath. The flask is heated by immersing it into tepid or boiling water up to the height of the material in the flask.

Figure 2: Balneum marie, Maria's Bath.

The **Second Degree** is a hotter temperature provided traditionally by an ash bath in which a pot of ashes is heated much like a pot of water. The flask to be heated is immersed up to the height of the material it contains.

The **Third Degree** is hotter still and is achieved with a sand or iron dust bath which is the same as the ash bath but uses sand or iron dust.

The **Fourth Degree** of Fire is the hottest that can be provided by a bare flame. A type of open flame is a "reverberating" flame, where the flame is reflected directly onto the matter being heated. The fire was traditionally a charcoal fire that was in a special furnace called an *athanor*. (See Figure 3, below.)

Figure 3: An athanor from Mutus Liber. *Altus. 1677.*

The athanor is the centerpiece of the alchemical laboratory, comparable to the heart and hearth of a home. It represents the central fire. The athanor, from the Arabic *al-tannur* (oven), was a simple brick or clay furnace shaped like a tower. Today heat is provided by electric hotplates and gas burners. True alchemical work can be done without a traditional athanor. But one should have one in one's heart and mind as heating and digestion go on.

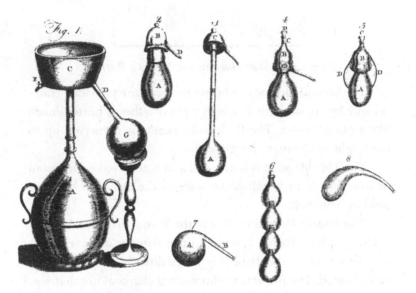

Figure 4: 1. Copper alembic. 2. Glass alembic.
3. Long-necked alembic. 4. One piece alembic. 5. Pelican.
6. Chain of aludels. 7 and 8. Retorts.
From Encyclopaedia Britannica, Vol. 2, 1771.

Other traditional alchemical tools included a variety of glass and ceramic ware designed to separate, purify, and recombine the Three Principles. (See Figure 4, above.) To calcine material, crucibles and iron pans were used. Distillation was achieved with a still. The alchemical still was made of two parts: the *alembic,* the part of the still that condenses vapor into a liquid, and the *curcurbite,* the lower part of the still that holds the liquid to be distilled. *Retorts* were also used for distillation. The *aludel,* an oval-shaped flask open at both ends was used in distillation to allow a more precise or "accurate" separation. It was placed between the curcurbite and the alembic to expand the vapors and to further separate the more volatile from the less volatile. The *Pelican* is a circulatory vessel. It has two side tubes that feed the condensed vapors back into the body.

In contemporary alchemy, ordinary laboratory glassware is used to achieve the same ends as these early tools. These pieces are listed in Appendix 1 along with a partial list of useful laboratory equipment.

Before proceeding to the work, there is a checklist of sorts. The first item is your motivation, or intention, then your understanding of the theories and goals of alchemy. And then there are the physical requirements of the practice as described by St. Albertus Magnus in his *Libellus de Alchimia:*

1. Silence. "The worker in this art must be silent and secretive." This is necessary to protect the Art from errors that can creep into the practice, the result being that "the secret will be lost and the work remain imperfect."

2. Place. The worker "should have a place and a special house, hidden from men," in which to do the work.

3. Time. "Observe the time in which the work must be done." He notes that, "sublimations are of little value in the winter."

4. Perseverance. "The worker in this art should be careful, and assiduous in his efforts . . . if he begins and does not persevere, he will lose both materials and time."

5. Rght Use. "It should be done according to the usage of art."

6. Glass. "All vessels in which medicines may be put . . . should be of glass or glazed."

7. Caution. "Be on one's guard before all else against associating oneself with princes or potentates." Albertus warns against associating one's work with "princes" because if you are not successful you will suffer, and if you are successful you will be detained, "ensnared by your own words and caught by your own discourses."

8. Funding. "No one should begin operations without plenty of funds," to complete the work, for with the work incomplete, time, material, everything, has been wasted.

Be very sure of them all. This path is an extremely demanding one and is not for the faint of heart, nor for those in search of spiritual fast food or spoon bending. It is a deep path, a challenging path, perhaps a bit foolish, and at times full of doubt. But yet . . .

CHAPTER EIGHT

THE PREPARATORY WORK

Where Nature ends, there the Art of man begins, for Nature's
ultimate matter is man's primal matter.[1]

—PARACELSUS

Water

A ll water should be distilled before being used in alchemical work unless otherwise noted. Water may be collected
from springs, rain, snow, or dew. Of these, dew, especially dew
collected in spring, and rain, especially rain collected during
a thunderstorm, are particularly valued due to the amount of
"fire" they hold. To collect the rain, place nonmetal buckets
outside during a heavy thunderstorm. Filter this water. Save
some undistilled for future use and distill the rest. It is best
stored in glass bottles.

The Grapevine

The root of alchemy is the grapevine. Without wine, vinegar,
and Salt of Tartar, all obtained from this noble plant, there
would be no alchemy. Much of alchemy stems from these
three. As all three can be obtained very easily, it is not crucial
to make your own wine and vinegar; even Salt of Tartar can be
obtained through art supply stores. But it is important to learn
how to ferment and calcine. And what better way than to work
with such a generous plant—the grapevine and all it can give.

Wine

Here is a brief overview of the wine-making process. It is not
very difficult and can be used to produce alcohol from any

plant. With a little care, study, and practice, one could actually end up with something quite good and drinkable.

Prepare the juice from pressed grapes, or if using plants, macerate them in water for a couple of days. The temperature should be 27°C. Sugar can be added to augment the naturally occurring sugars in the plant or the grape mash. The yeast is then added, and the temperature is maintained between 21°C and 24°C. Primary fermentation now takes place. The temperature should be kept below 29.5°C. The mixture is stirred twice a day to break up the cap that forms on top. Check the temperature and cool or warm accordingly. When the violent fermentation stops, draw off the liquid and press the pulp to expel all liquid. Keep about 15 percent of the solution separate for topping up. Secondary fermentation now begins. Add the fermentation lock.[2] This allows the gas to escape without allowing air in. After three weeks draw off the wine from the sediment and top up from the 15 percent you set aside. To get the most alcohol, this process can be repeated two more times with three-month intervals and then a final time with a six-month fermentation period. Wine is typically about 12 percent alcohol.[3] The alcohol may be distilled off as soon as the first secondary fermentation is done. This wine can be distilled to obtain the spirit, or it may be used to make vinegar.

Vinegar

To make vinegar is a very simple thing. Just set up some very simple conditions and Nature does the rest. Take wine and dilute it to 5–7 percent alcohol. Pour three parts of wine into a sanitized glass or stoneware container, filling it less than two-thirds full and add one part of vinegar culture[4] with active bacteria. Store it in a dark place and keep it at a temperature between 27°C and 29.5°C. A film will form on top of the liquid. This is the "mother." At 24°C–27°C it will take approximately six to eight weeks for conversion to vinegar.[5] New wine should be added to the culture every four to eight weeks depending on the conversion rate. Add new alcohol below the "mother." It is important not to disturb this layer. Adding more alcohol to the culture keeps it alive. When all the alcohol is converted to vinegar (an acid test will determine this), draw off the vinegar and pasteurize it and filter it. Vinegar is 5 percent acetic acid.

Keep some of the vinegar unpasteurized to be used to start other cultures. The vinegar is ready for use as is or for distillation.

If you wish to remove the coloring from red wine vinegar, take, for every liter of vinegar, 50 grams of bone charcoal and mix together in a glass vessel. Stir often and in several days the coloring will be absorbed by the charcoal, leaving the vinegar clear.

Salt of Tartar

Salt of Tartar, also known as potash or pearl ash, is potassium carbonate. It is the most common salt in land plants. The Salt of Tartar opens many doors in alchemy and is prepared by taking dried grapevine or oak wood, or even better, raw tartar[6] from oak wine barrels. Calcine it, that is, burn it to an ash. The ash is mixed with distilled rainwater dissolving the Salt of Tartar. Heating the solution and stirring ensures that as much of the salt as possible is dissolved. This is also called *leaching*. The solution is then filtered. This may be repeated several times to be sure all the salt has been leached out. Put all the filtered liquids together and evaporate the water by heating it, but do not allow it to boil. Once it is evaporated, collect the damp salts and calcine again, and again dissolve in hot water, filter, and evaporate. Repeat until all the salts are pure and then calcine one final time to drive off all excess water. Be careful not to melt the salts. You should have at this point a very white or even bluish salt. This is the Salt of Tartar, and it is very hydroscopic. Store it in an airtight and moisture-proof container. Salt of Tartar attacks glass, so try using glazed ceramic containers to store it. This process maybe used on any plant to obtain its salt.

CHAPTER NINE

THE ART OF DISTILLATION

L et us take what we have so far—water, wine, vinegar, and Salt of Tartar—and move them up a notch, so to speak, and from them prepare distilled water, Spirit of Wine, distilled vinegar and finish the rest of the preparation for alchemical work. The main technique used to this end is distillation.

Distilled Water

Distillation (see Appendix 1 for technique and equipment) is a form of purification, separating the subtle from the gross.

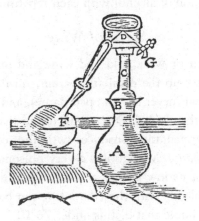

Figure 5

Water is placed into a flask (A) (see Figure 5), and it is then heated to a boil (100°C). The water vapor rises through (C) to (D) where the steam collects and condenses back into liquid water due to the cooling effect of the cold water in (E). The liquid water, the distillate, drains down into a separate flask (F); any impurities will be left behind in the boiling flask. This distillation is a good illustration of the rotation of the elements. We take Water, cold and wet, increase the heat, changing it to hot and wet, or steam vapor, that is, Air. We then transfer the heat from the Air to the cold water in (E) causing Air: hot and wet, to condense into Water: cold and wet, leaving any Earth behind.

Distillation is also used to separate mixed liquids from each other, exploiting the difference in boiling points between liquids. For example, distilling alcohol from wine takes advantage of the fact that water boils at 100°C while alcohol boils at 78.5°C. By keeping the temperature at around 80°C–85°C, we are able to separate the alcohol from the water. Of course some water does come over, so the distillate, the liquid that comes over, is actually about 50 percent alcohol. This was first discovered by the Arab alchemists and mentioned by such alchemists as al-Kindi (ninth century A.D.). This alcohol solution was called *aqua ardens* and *aqua vitae* by Arnold Villanova around 1300 A.D. It may be taken and distilled, thus increasing the concentration of alcohol with each repetition.

Spirit of Wine

To make Spirit of Wine, take red wine and put into a distillation flask, set up the distillation train, turn on cold water, turn on the heat (never use an open flame), and distill over the spirit, that is the alcohol. Discard all liquid that distills under 76°C. Plant fermentation produces two kinds of alcohols, *ethanol* and *methanol*. Methanol is a very poisonous compound, but because of its low boiling point (64°C) and the fact that it does not "blend" with the ethanol, it can be eliminated by discarding all liquid that distills under 76°C.

The first distillation of the wine may be done at a temperature of 80°C. This yields a distillate that is 50 to 60 percent alcohol. This is the *aqua vitae* of Villanova and can be used in the preparation of herbal tinctures. Subsequent distillations done more precisely at a temperature of 78.5°C (the boiling point of ethanol) will yield the sharp spirit called the "Spirit of Wine." The highest concentration you can achieve is 95 percent, due to the hydroscopic nature of alcohol. If you did achieve a concentration higher than this, the alcohol would very quickly suck water vapor from the air until it was at a 95 percent concentration. The last remaining water can be removed by using calcined Salt of Tartar. The resulting spirit is called Rectified Spirit of Wine.

Rectified Spirit of Wine

To rectify the Spirit of Wine, take Spirit of Wine and Salt of Tartar that has been calcined for at least one hour at 350°C. This heating can be done in an ordinary oven; drying the Salt of Tartar allows it to absorb the remaining water in the Spirit of Wine. Mix one part of the Salt of Tartar with four parts of the Spirit of Wine and let it macerate for one day, allowing the potassium carbonate to draw the water to itself. Shake from time to time, but keep it closed so that water vapor from the atmosphere doesn't enter the flask. Then distill. The final distillate is the Rectified Spirit of Wine.

The percentage of alcohol can be increased through subsequent distillations with calcined Salt of Tartar with a lesser proportion of tartar to Spirit of Wine, that is, one part calcined tartar to six parts Spirit of Wine followed by a further distillation over calcined tartar at a proportion of 25 g calcined tartar to 1000 ml Spirit of Wine. With the use of moisture traps, the percentage of alcohol can get as high as 99.5 percent. Storage at this level of purity is extremely difficult due to the hydroscopic nature of alcohol, so Spirit of Wine rectified to this point should be used immediately.

Distilled Vinegar

The purification of vinegar, the making of a concentrated acetic acid, may be done through both congelation (freezing) and distillation. We shall focus on distillation. Ventilation is very important as you will be distilling an acid. Acetic acid boils at 118°C and water at 100°C, so in this distillation, water, and water with varying amounts of acetic acid, will come over first as the temperature increases. The first fraction to come over at 100°C is mostly water. The second fraction comes over starting at 103°C peaking at 105°C. Save the first and second fractions and keep separately. These have acetic acid in them that can be recovered with subsequent distillation. Switch receivers when the temperature is around 105°C. The third fraction comes over between 105°C and 118°C and is mostly acetic acid. Distill carefully.

Do not burn and do not distill to dryness but keep distilling until what is left behind has the consistency of honey. The distillate is the distilled vinegar. You can redistill the distillate until the concentration of the acetic acid is 80 percent. For most of the work with metals, an acetic acid concentration of 20 percent to 30 percent is sufficient. Determine the acetic concentration by using a hydrometer.[1]

Since vinegar is 5 percent acetic acid, to obtain 1 liter of 80 percent acetic acid you will need to start with 16 liters of red wine vinegar. This is almost 4 gallons of liquid to distill, with 95 percent of it water. An easy way to remove the bulk of the water is to freeze the vinegar before distillation, thus concentrating it to a smaller more manageable volume.

To concentrate the vinegar by freezing, take red wine vinegar and fill a bottle halfway. Lay the bottle on its side so the mouth of the container is clear of any liquid. Let it freeze (vinegar at 5 percent acetic acid freezes at -3°C). Freezing the vinegar at this angle allows better drainage for the melting acetic acid. Once the entire liquid is frozen solid, take the bottle and tip it upside down into a collection flask or bottle. The acetic acid will melt first (melting point: 16.7°C) and run red into the flask or bottle. Collect this runoff in several fractions until the block of ice in the original bottle is white and colorless. This shows that only water remains. Dispose of the ice.

Take these various fractions and freeze again and cycle through the freezing and draining, concentrating the acetic acid until you have a manageable volume and are ready to distill.

CHAPTER TEN

THE PURIFICATION OF SALTS:
CALCINATION, CRYSTALLIZATION, AND SUBLIMATION

Calcination

See page 57, Salt of Tartar.

Crystallization

Crystallization is a balance between solid and liquid. Too much water yields a solution; too little water leaves a brittle material. With the right proportion of water, the salt and water lock up and a crystal is formed. This water, necessary for crystallization, is often referred to as the "water of crystallization." With the application of heat to the crystal, the water is turned to air, drying the crystal, collapsing it into dust. Again we see an example of the rotation of the elements.

To crystallize any soluble salt, first dissolve the salt to be crystallized in distilled water. Heat to 45–50°C and make a saturated solution by adding more of the salt, shaking and stirring, until no more will dissolve. Let it sit for an hour or so then decant into another flask and keep heating. When small crystals begin to form, remove the solution from the heat and cool.

To grow beautiful crystals, take a portion of the prepared solution and pour it into a beaker to about 3 cm deep. Cover it loosely with foil or a paper towel and set it aside until the crystals have grown to around 2 cm to 5 cm long. Add more solution as needed. Once the crystals are at the desired size, decant the solution back into the stock saturated solution. Select the best-looking crystals and put each one in its own beaker of solution 3 cm deep. Once a day, carefully and gently turn over the crystal. If other crystals start to form, decant the smaller crystals and the solution back into the stock solution. Isolate the large crystal and add more solution to cover the crystal.

Sublimation

Some salts, when heated, do not pass through a liquid phase but turn directly to gas, leaving whatever impurities behind. When this gas is cooled, it condenses directly into a solid. By repeating this process several times, a salt with this property, such as sal ammoniac (NH_4Cl), is purified.

To sublimate sal ammoniac, first make sure you have adequate ventilation. The gas produced is very toxic. Do not breathe the vapors.

Take the sal ammoniac and crush it finely. Place an even layer (no more than 2 cm thick) of the powder in a Pyrex dish and cover it with the glass cover. Heat the salt (sal ammoniac sublimates at 520°C) until it sublimates on the bottom of the lid, leaving a deposit about 1 inch thick. This sublimate is the purified sal ammoniac. Scrape this off and sublimate it again. Once more, take what sublimated on the lid and repeat until there is no black residue and all the salt sublimes. To purify sal ammoniac, it is necessary to sublimate the salt at least three times. If the salt is yellow, it is a good sign. This is then triple-sublimed sal ammoniac and will be used throughout the work.

CHAPTER ELEVEN

FURTHER WORK WITH WATER AND ALCOHOL

Archaeus of Water

*A*rchaeus, from the Greek *archeios*, a ruler, is a term coined by Paracelsus to denote the sense of a vital force and an agent of direction. The Archaeus of Water is this vital force and agency of water. It is made manifest or freed through the separation and purification of the Four Elements and the subsequent separation and purification of their Three Principles, followed by the recombination of the principles and then the elements.

Creating the Archaeus of Water is a very good introduction to the Four Elements and the practice of purification through the art of distillation while producing a very active and potent form of water.

Take two liters of rainwater collected during a thunderstorm or dew. Put it into a flask and cover the mouth of the flask with filter paper to allow it to breathe while keeping dust out. Put the flask in a warm place for one month, allowing it to putrefy. Set up the distillation apparatus. Distill in 500 ml portions using an aludel to allow for maximum expansion of the elements. The first 500 ml portion to come over is the element Fire, followed by Air, then by Water, and the last 500 ml to come over is Earth. The residue left behind in the distillation flask will look like a spongy, slimy mass. Save this and gently dry it. It has been called the "true universal gur."[1] It allegedly has some health benefits, but these need to be investigated.

Each of the four Elemental portions is then further distilled into three fractions (166.66 ml each) for each of the Three

Principles. The principles come over in order of their volatility, first Mercury, then Sulfur, and finally Salt. At the end of the distillation, you will have twelve, 166.66 ml portions of distilled water. You will have Mercury of Fire, Sulphur of Fire, Salt of Fire; Mercury of Air, Sulphur of Air, Salt of Air, and so on.

The twelve portions are now recombined by principles of a particular element to recreate the original Element. For example, pour the Mercury of Earth into the Salt of Earth then add the Sulfur of Earth.

This is then the Earth element reconstituted. Reconstitute all the Elements in this manner. Then take the Elements and mix first Earth, Water, Air, then Fire. Once fully reconstituted it is now the Archaeus of Water. This is a highly potentized water.[2] Although we started with putrefied rainwater, any water will be greatly improved with this process.

Oil of Tartar per deliquium (oleum tartari p.d.)

Place Salt of Tartar well calcined in a nonmetallic bowl; glazed ceramic is best. Place the bowl at least 1 foot off the ground in a cellar or some other moist place until it is resolved into an oil (this is preferably done in the spring). Filter and store in a nonmetallic, nonglass container. This is the Oil of Tartar and is used in making the *primum ens* of herbs. If this oil is then filtered and distilled, one can obtain *Angel Water,* which can be used in the extraction of essences.

Spirit of Wine of the Sages

To make this spirit, according to a 1655 work diary of Sir Robert Boyle, one should "Take spirit of wine & Salt armoni-acke finely powder'd drive them over in a Retort till the Spirit (by some Cohobations) be sufficiently impregnated with the Salt."[3] Dr. Theodore Kerckringius, in his 1678 translation of *The Triumphal Chariot of Antimony,*[4] gives the following spec-ifications: Mix four ounces of sublimed sal ammoniac, into ten ounces of rectified spirits of wine. Digest in a flask until the

Spirit of Wine is filled with the "fire or sulphur of the salt of ammonia." Check for color changes during the two phases of the lunar cycle. Cohobate three times. This is the Spirit of Wine of the Sages. Frater Albertus called it *Kerckringius Menstruum*, in honor of Dr. Kerckringius.

CHAPTER TWELVE

THE HERBAL WORK

It is a wise thing to begin our work by starting with herbs for several reasons. Aside from the obvious reason of wanting to make some very potent alchemical herbal preparations, there is the reason of experience and understanding gained in working with materials that are more forgiving. This experience and a deeper understanding of alchemical theory is an essential foundation for further more intricate work.

Let us review the theory of the Three Principles and apply it to the Plant Kingdom.

Like all things, plants can be analyzed in terms of the Three Principles of Mercury, Sulphur, and Salt.

Mercury—Spirit—Alcohol

Obtained through the fermentation of the plant's sugars by yeast. The Mercury is the same throughout the plant kingdom, since all sugars are converted to alcohol through the fermentation process. Mercury is a subtle matrix within which reside Sulphur and Salt.

Sulphur—Soul—Essential Oil

Obtained through the distillation or the pressing of a plant. The Sulphur is unique to the particular species of plant. Sulphur is the matrix within which the Mercury resides.

Salt—Body—Mineral Salts

Obtained through the calcinations of the plant matter. The Salts are made up of various mineral salts in varying proportions, with potassium carbonate in the greatest proportion. The Salt is the matrix within which the Sulphur resides.

Mercury, Sulphur, and Salt are three interpenetrating matrices. Each is dependent on the others in creating and maintaining the plant.

The herbal work consists of separating the Principles, purifying them, and then recombining them. This process is also called *spagyry, spagyria,* or *spagyrics,* from the Greek *span,* "to tear open," and *ageirein,* "to collect," "to combine." This is done through a variety of means, each producing a different end product. You can use these preparations much as you would the herb it was produced from. These alchemical products are much more potent and intensified, so care should be taken in their use.

Spagyric Tinctures

A spagyric tincture is an alcohol extract of a plant that utilizes all three of the plant's purified Principles, that is: the Mercury, Sulphur and Salt.

Here are two methods to make the spagyric tincture of an herb. The first is based on a standard procedure for making herbal tinctures. The other is adapted from the *Art of Distillation*[1] by John French.

1. Take an herb and macerate it in a 50:50 alcohol:water solution for two weeks. This alcohol solution can be *aqua vitae,* distilled from wine or, more readily, vodka. Filter, press the mass to squeeze every last drop out of the herb, and save the solution. Calcine the remaining vegetable solids until they are an ash. Next either add the ash to the solution, circulate for a week, and then filter; or take the ash and extract and purify its Salt of Tartar, then add this to the tincture. This second level of purification for this type of tincture is not necessary as long as the ash is adequately filtered from the tincture.

2. Take a fresh herb and chop it up. Add water, yeast, and sugar (not necessary but it will give a higher alcohol content) to the freshly chopped herb and set it to ferment. When no more gas is produced, the fermentation is over. Using an aludel, distill very gently. Distill until there are two parts distillate for every part of fresh herb used. To the distillate add enough pure Mercury to bring the concentration up to at least 15 percent. Take the remaining vegetable matter and calcine it. Purify the salts and add them to the tincture. Since this is a more refined spagyric tincture, it is best to purify the salts first, before adding them to the tincture.

A spagyric tincture differs from the usual herbal tincture in that the spagyric tinctures contain the plant salts that complete the full therapeutic profile of the plant in question.

Tinctures should be made from herbs for each of the seven planets. In Appendix 2 there is a brief list of some of the more useful and interesting herbs and their planetary rulership to help select an appropriate herb.

The Herbal Magistry

A Magistry is the medicinal virtue of a substance, in this case an herb, preserved in a vehicle.

Take 0.5 kg of the herb and macerate in 2 liters of water for 1–3 days. Maceration helps to break down the plant and releases the oils. When ready to distill off the essential oil, add more water to bring the volume up to the desired level (2 liters). Distill the oil. See Appendix 1 for the techniques and equipment needed for distillation. Separate the oil and keep it in a dark glass bottle. Letting the distillation flask and the remaining material cool down and "rest" for twelve to twenty-four hours and then continuing distillation, more of the Sulphur can be extracted. Note that the bulk of the Sulphur comes over in the first distillation, so it becomes a question of time and efficiency whether to continue distilling. Collect all the bottles and put them together in one. This is the Sulphur.

Take the remaining mixture and adjust the temperature to 27°C. Add the yeast starter and sugar and let it ferment. When fermentation is complete, strain the mixture and put the mass aside for calcinations. Take the liquid and distill out the Spirit. Rectify the Spirit and keep it in a glass bottle. This is the Mercury.

Take the remaining liquid and solids and calcine them to ash. They can be calcined separately or together. The remaining liquid when evaporated and calcined will yield the Salt of Sulphur. The solids when calcined will give the Salt of Salt.

Since the two salts will ultimately be mixed together, I take the whole mix of liquid and solid and calcine them together. Take the ash from this calcination and dissolve, filter, and evaporate it; repeat this until the salts are as pure as possible. If you processed the two salts separately, they should be recombined at this point. This is the Salt.

Take the 500 ml Mercury, all the Sulphur, and all the Salt and mix them. Add some of the Mercury to the Salts, just enough to dissolve them, then add all the Sulphur. Add more Mercury if it seems necessary to keep the Salt and the Sulphur in solution. Seal them in a flask and let them digest for one month at 40°C and then circulate for an additional one month. Add more Mercury if necessary to keep the Salt and the Sulphur in solution.

This is the Magistry of the selected herb, i.e., the medicinal virtue of the particular herb in a particular vehicle, that is, the Mercury, alcohol. It has all the virtues of the plant purified and intensified. It is a 1:1 tincture by weight:volume. In this case it is 500 grams of dried herb to 500 ml of solvent.

Alternatively one could work with Mercury distilled from wine instead of going through the fermentation process, as well as work with commercially distilled essential oils (as long as they are steam distilled and no other extraction method has been used).

Like the tinctures, Magistries for each of the seven planets should be made up.

Spagyric Plant Stone

The Three Principles can be combined so that the Salt and the Sulphur predominate to give rise to the spagyric plant stone. This Vegetable Stone is a hard wax-like substance that is the result of the successful separation, purification, combination, and digestion of the Three Principles. The Stone cannot form a separation like the *circulatum minus* can effect (see page 80), but it has all the virtues of the plant from which it was made. And it is far more energetic and efficacious than the raw herb, having been freed from superfluous and impure material.

The Vegetable Stone can take on an appearance from an almost tarlike substance to a fully digested, hard wax-like, translucent stone. Regardless of its outward form, if it has been properly combined, the virtues of the plant, whether medicinal, initiatic, or other, will be intensified.

To make the Vegetable Stone, take the Salt, Sulphur, and Mercury of a plant as prepared in the Magistry (or commercially obtained). Combine and digest them. There are several ways to achieve this.

One way is the Salts are added to the Mercury and circulated and digested at 40°C. This is then the matrix to which the Sulphur is added, circulated, and digested. It is then gently distilled. Repeat this process of adding Mercury and Sulphur until the Salt has absorbed all the Sulphur and Mercury it can.

The other, and I think better, order of combination is to add the Sulphur to the Salt first. This allows for volatilization of some of the Salt before being absorbed and dispersed throughout the Mercury. The Salt should also be very well calcined and heated for an hour before use to ensure all the water has been driven off. Remember, oil and water do not mix. Water will prevent an intimate mix from occurring.

Place the heated Salt evenly in a flask and add the Sulphur to cover the Salt in slight excess. Seal the flask and incubate at

40°C for one week. If the Salt is dry, add more Sulphur. When the amount of Sulphur floating on top of the Salt is the same as what has been put in, the Salt has taken all the Sulphur it can and will take on a waxy, slimy appearance.

Add enough of the Mercury to cover the Salt and Sulphur mixture in slight excess. Digest and then add more Mercury until the Salt cannot absorb any more.

A third method is to make a mixture of one part Mercury and one part Sulphur. This mixture is then added to the purified Salt so that a thin layer (one centimeter high) floats above the Salt. Digest and circulate this for one week. This is repeated until, during calcinations, the Salt melts like wax without smoking.

If any of these methods produces a waxy substance that appears to be a "stone," take a piece of it and test it by seeing if it can be dissolved in water. If it dissolves in water, use a higher proportion of Sulphur to Mercury, and cycle through two or three more calcinations and imbibitions, circulations and digestions until the substance does not dissolve in water. It is the Sulphur that holds the stone together. It is the Soul that allows for the union of Spirit and Body.

Grinding and calcining the Stone gently, and repeating the process with more of the Sulphur and Mercury, can increase its virtue. The more this is repeated, the more potent the Stone becomes. This Stone has all the virtues of the plant but at a more energetic level.

Regardless of the order that the three Principles were combined, place the Stone in an incubator and digest for six months to a year until it is solid. This is the Vegetable Stone.

If the plant in question has little or no volatile oil, a tincture is extracted by macerating the plant in Rectified Spirit of Wine. The liquid extracted is a mixture of the Sulphur and the Mercury. Distill off the Mercury that has now become "determined" through its intimate contact with the plant. This is saved for use in the recombination of the principles. Distilled water is added to the remaining greenish liquid and is then digested in a water bath at about 80°C until the water becomes a very intense red. Let the solution cool and then filter. The water contains the organic salts of the plant. Evaporate it very slowly; it will either turn into a honey-like syrup or it will crystallize. Dissolve and recrystallize to purify the Salt of Sulphur.

If the Salt of Sulphur has formed crystals, then take equal weights of Salt of Sulphur and Salt and mix them well, then imbibe with the determined Mercury. If the Salt of Sulphur is a honey-like consistency, then dissolve the Salt of Sulphur with the determined Mercury and then imbibe the Salt with this mixture. Follow the above procedures for finishing the Stone.

Another method of working with plants with little Sulphur is by way of Oil of Tartar. Paracelsus referred to extracts made in this way as being the *ens*. The *ens* is the essential healing aspect of a plant—its virtue. One famous *ens* is the *primum ens Melissae*, the *ens* of Lemon Balm *(Melissa officinalis)*. Lemon Balm is an herb with very little Sulphur.

Primum Ens Melissae

Primum ens—the first extract of mineral natures is the *Primum ens*. It is the first matter, the seat of life and motion. With a fresh infusion of vitality provided by the *ens,* the human body can be rejuvenated.

In his biography of Paracelsus, Franz Hartman quotes Paracelsus on the creation of the *primum ens Melissae,* a very potent and rejuvenating material derived from the herb Lemon Balm, an herb with very little essential oil. Hartman quotes Lesebure, a physician of Louis XIV of France, who gives the following report as to the use and effect of the *primum ens Melissae*:

> First he took, every morning at sunrise, a glass of white wine that was tinctured with this remedy, and after using it for fourteen days his finger- and toe-nails began to fall out, without however, causing any pain. He was not courageous enough to continue

the experiment, but gave the same remedy to the old female servant. She took it every morning for about ten days, when she began to menstruate again as in former days. At this she was very much surprised, because she did not know that she had been taking a medicine. She became frightened, and refused to continue the experiment. My friend took, therefore, some grain, soaked it in that wine, and gave it to the old hen to eat, and on the sixth day that bird began to lose its feathers, and kept losing them until it was perfectly nude, but before two weeks had passed, new feathers grew, which were much more beautifully colored; her comb stood up again, and she began again to lay eggs.[2]

Here is the description of the process. This procedure may be used in general to extract the *ens* from any herb. It is particularly useful in plants with little essential oil.

Cover fresh Lemon Balm *(Melissa officinalis)* leaves with the Oil of Tartar (see page 66). Seal the flask and digest. In twenty-four to forty-eight hours, the Oil of Tartar will have extracted a tincture from the herb. Draw off this tincture from the leaves and discard the leaves.

On top of this liquid pour very sharp Mercury so that it covers the liquid 2–5 cm deep. When the Mercury becomes intensely tinged, take it away, save it, and put fresh Mercury upon the alkaline liquid. Repeat until the Mercury absorbs all the color. This may take one to three months.

This tincture is then gently distilled until the tincture in the flask begins to thicken. Stop the distillation at this point. Pour the thickening tincture into an evaporation dish and allow the remaining alcohol to evaporate, until it becomes the thickness of syrup. This is the *primum ens Melissae*. The distilled alcohol can be reused. Alternatively the tincture can be left as is after it is drawn off, and this is then the Tincture of *primum ens Melissae*.

The ens should be prepared for each planet. The following is a good selection of herbs to work with. Most of these herbs, like Lemon Balm, have a very low Sulphur content. They are also all rather friendly and healthful. But before use, make sure you know the use and benefits of the herbs as well as your own physical state.

The Moon—Hyssop
Mercury—Savory
Venus—Lady's mantle
The Sun—Rose damask
Mars—Basil
Jupiter—Lemon balm
Saturn—Horsetail

Volatilized Salts of Tartar

The volatilization of Salt was one of the major problems of the alchemists—how to make the fixed fly. The fixed, the Salt in this case, is almost always the Salt of Tartar. Instead of just presenting the procedure, I will use this as an example of a way to approach a question. The question here is not only "how is the Salt of Tartar volatized?" but also, perhaps more philosophically, "how is the fixed made to fly?"

To begin to open this question, first collect into one place all mentions of the process under investigation—here it is the volatilization of Salt. At the same time discover the emblems, images, and metaphors the alchemists used for the volatilization of the fixed. Read across the processes and look for what they hold in common. Look for what the overall shape and flow of the process is. Begin to reproduce some of the visual images you have found. Use these images as a support for your meditations on the process. Find the inner resonances with whatever spiritual tradition you are working within. Each aspect begins to reinforce the other, and slowly, the contradictions are resolved, and the path becomes clear. I will give here only the physical processes, leaving the more subtle inner work to you.

Johann van Helmont, *Ortus Medicinae.* 1648.
Dissolve Salt of Tartar in warm wine vinegar and set it to digest in a warm place for 40 days. Remove the vinegar and a clear crystalline salt will remain. Dissolve this salt in distilled rainwater and filter several times. Evaporate the water and a clear snow-white salt remains. From this salt distill by water water-bath a spirit. Once the spirit has been removed, let the salt sit for another month in a sand bath. The salt will sublime and fix itself to the sides of the glass. This is the Volatilized Salt of Tartar.[3]

Sir Robert Boyle. Work Note Books 1655 BP 8 fol 141v. Item 20.
To make Elixir Salis volatilis, Rx Essentiall oyle 2. Parts, pure Salt of tartar one part (Stirke[4] sometimes told me he tooke 3 parts of oyl & two of salt) & let them circulate with a Bottome heat 3 or 4 months. The salt will be like sugar-candy & somewhat tincted by the oyle, & will sticke to the sides of the Glasse (which must be large & strong, & exquisitely stopt with Helmont's Lute ex cerâ & colephoniâ) at the Bottom of which not withstanding som liquor will remaine. Stirkius.

Item 89.
Take Sal tartari very moist but not enough to be a Lixivium & imbibe it by degrees with a chymicall oyle, beating & working them very well together in a fit Mortar; then spread them thinly in a Platter, & leave them sub dio. And in few (3, 4, or most commonly 7 or 8) dayes it will be a candy, which may be afterwards imbibed with new oyle (& handled as before) till it be satiated. NB. 1. Dr St. tooke a pound of oyle of Mint (Speake-mint) as much Salt of Mint & as much of the herbe it selfe & beate them into lozenges (broade & thin) which by degrees sub dio turned altogether into

Candy. 2. These Candys by cohobations with pure spirit of wine will passe thorough the Retort, leaving only behind a resinous substance liquable in Water &c.

Encyclopedia Brittanica. 1771. Vol. 2, p. 154. *To Combine Essential Oils with Fixed Alkalis.*
Take salt of tartar, or any other alkali; thoroughly calcined. Heat it in a crucible till it be red, and in that condition throw it into a hot iron mortar: rub it quickly with a very hot iron pestle; and as soon as it is powdered, pour on it, little by little, nearly an equal quantity of oil of turpentine. The oil will enter into the salt, and unite intimately with it, so as to form a hard paste. Continue rubbing this composition with a pestle, in order to complete the union of the two substances; and, as your oil of turpentine disappears, add more, which will unite in the same manner, and give a softer consistency to the soapy mass.

Starkey's method of mixing and waiting was more tedious. This faster method is accredited to a Dr. Geoffroy.

In examining these formulae we find that the main thing they hold in common is that some liquid acts on the Salt of Tartar. The liquids are either distilled vinegar or an essential oil, both of which are comprised of organic acids.

In general, to volatilize alkaline mineral salts, use organic acids, either acetic acid or the organic acids found in resins or volatile oils. Essential oil, simply added to Salt of Tartar and digested, volatilizes the salt. Improvements to the process include heating the salt to assure its dryness and keeping it hot while adding the Sulphur.

Tartar is also volatilized through cohobation with distilled vinegar. Add distilled vinegar to the Salt of Tartar, and the tartar will effervesce. Keep adding vinegar until the salt is saturated and the fizzing has stopped. Place this mixture in a flask and prepare for a distillation by sand bath. Distill with a gentle heat very slowly until nothing remains but a dry matter. Add a little of the vinegar until the salt is saturated and distill again to dryness.[5] The remaining solid is semivolatile. Sublime the salts. This sublimated salt is the Volatile Salt of Tartar.

Knowing this, go back over the processes and start to determine a work plan. And then actually do the work. As you work, bring to mind the various images you've been working with and see how they relate to the process in front of you and to each other. Then compare your results to the original texts from which this process was drawn. How does it compare to your experiment? Was something missed? Experience with volatilizing salts is valuable in understanding alchemy, and it is key to the next work, the *circulatum minus*—a truly alchemical creature.

The Circulatum Minus

A circulatum is simply any medium or solvent that can be used and recovered to be used again. Paracelsus wrote about these throughout his work. But it is a short tract by Baro Urbigerus, written in 1691, that draws our attention. In this brief work he gives very explicit directions in the composition of just such a circulatum, which he calls the *circulatum minus*—the lesser circulation. This circulatum is able to quickly extract the Three Principles from a fresh plant immersed in it. Within moments of being immersed in this liquid, the Sulphur, along with some of the Salt, begins to bubble up and float to the surface. Here, concentrated, are all the medicinal virtues of the immersed plant.

In his tract, Urbigerus outlines three possible methods for its cre-ation. The methods differ really only in how the start-ing materials, the Three Principles, were arrived at—the first is done "philosophically" without "addition"; the second, by way of the grape, "a Plant of the noblest Degree"; the third and the one I outline here, is with commercially prepared material. But the process they are put through is the same for each.

The overall process is as follows: The Sulphur is blended with the Salt to volatilize it. More Sulphur is added until the Salt is saturated. This mixture is then circulated with highly rectified spirits of wine and digested. It is then distilled and cohobated at least seven times. The final distillation yields the *circulatum minus*. Having given, in the most general of terms, an outline of the process and the work, I will give the procedure explicitly laid out from practical experience.

THE THIRD METHOD OF BARO URBIGERUS
FOR PREPARING THE CIRCULATUM MINUS

VI. The third and common way is only a Conjunction of a fixt Vegetable Salt with its own volatil sulphureous Spirit, both to be found ready prepared by any vulgar Chymist, and since in their Preparation the purest Sulphur, containing the Soul, has suffered some Detriment by their not being philosophically manipulated, they cannot be inseparably joined without a sulphureous Medium, by which the Soul being strengthened, the Body and Spirit are also through it made capable of a perfect Union.

VII. The proper Medium, requisite for the indissoluble Union of these two Subjects, is only a sulphureous and bituminous Matter, issuing out of a plant, living or dead, which is to be found in several parts of the World, and is known to all manner of sea fishermen (the Copavian we find to be the best, and after that the Italian), by which, after it has been separated from its feculent parts through our Universal Menstruum, all the Pores and Atoms of the fixt Vegetable Salt, which is extremely fortified by it, being dilated, it is made capable of receiving its own Spirit, and uniting itself with it.[6]

The medium that allows for the use of commercially obtained materials, the "sulphureous and bituminous Matter," is a resin[7] known to all manner of "sea fishermen." Let us consider the term "sea fishermen." Not just a sea-goer but a fisherman, one who fishes by the sea. There is a tree that grows along the southern European seashores known variously by its common names as maritime pine, sea pine, or ocean pine. Its botanical name is *pinus pilaster,*[8] and it is the source of oil of tere-binth, that is, oil of turpentine. It is this oil that George Starkey found to be the most effective essential oil with which to volatilize the Salt of Tartar. Urbigerus mentions that Copavia balsam is the best followed by the Italian pine. Practically speaking, any balsam should be able to be used, and in fact success has been had using Canada balsam, the oleoresin obtained from *Abies balsamea,* Cypress, and others. The important thing is that the resin used has its naturally occurring organic acids still present, for it is these acids that allow the Salt to volatilize.

The materials needed for this method are: 1. the Salts of the plant, purified and calcined or commercially obtained Salt of Tartar (potassium carbonate) also calcined; 2. the Sulphur, that is, the essential oil of a plant. If the oil is obtained commercially make sure it is steam distilled and not solvent extracted; 3. To augment the "weakened"[9] Sulphur, a balsam is used. Any of the above will do or any other such balsams that one would care to experiment with; and 4. the Mercury, a highly rectified Spirit of Wine.

For 500 ml of *circulatum minus* you need about 20 grams of the Salt, 25 ml of the Sulphur, 35 ml of balsam, and 500 ml of Mercury. This is only a rough guide as to how much of the material you should have at hand.

Moisten the Salt with the Sulphur until it is just wet. Then, little by little, add the balsam, grinding and mixing it all to a honey-like consistency. Do this at 40°C. I find that using a mortar and pestle under a bell jar allows easy access for grinding and stirring. Use all the Sulphur and all the Salts, and then add a bit more of the resin. It should have the consistency of honey. Digest the mixture at 40°C. When the mixture becomes dry, reimbibe with more resin. Stir frequently nine to ten times a day. Exposure to air seems to be helpful in the volatilization of the Salt, so do the imbibition and digestion in a rather large stoppered flask. In three to four weeks, the Salt should be fully saturated and should have a slimy, glassy appearance and feel soapy to the touch. This is the most important part of the process. This is when the volatilization of the Salt takes place.

When the Salt is ready, eight parts of the rectified Mercury are added to one part of the Salt/Sulphur/balsam mixture. Let the mix putrefy for eight to ten days; stir it daily. You should notice a change of color, and the Salt will appear like slime at the bottom of the flask. Circulate for one week.

Distill carefully—do not let the resin come over or allow it to burn. Cohobate, i.e., pour the distillate back over the remaining mixture in the flask. Additional digestions may be useful. Repeat this cycle of distillation and cohobation for a total of seven times. Then do the final distillation. This distillate has a very sharp odor. It is the *circulatum minus*.

To test it, take a few leaves from a fresh plant and immerse it in your solution. A proper circulatum will separate out the Three Principles in less than fifteen minutes depending on the strength.[10]

After reading through this procedure, go back and review the section on the volatilization of Salts. You will notice that Sir Robert Boyle in item 89 is describing a similar process of using the essential oil to volatilize the Salt and using the Spirit of Wine to carry it over.

It is important to try to understand the underlying processes and not just slavishly follow recipes. The mastery of the *circulatum minus* is the basis for future work. There is no pretending at success, no possibility of self-delusion about success. What you end up with at the end of the process either works or it doesn't. What one learns and gains in the process is a foundation much in the way the circulatum itself is a foundation for the work.

One final note: This process is very simple but rather tricky. Be prepared for several attempts before succeeding. But realize that even in failure, experience is gained. Furthermore, while the distillate may not be the *circulatum minus,* it is still a wonderful and refined spagyric tincture.

CHAPTER THIRTEEN

PLANTS AS MEDICINES AND INITIATORY SUBSTANCES

All things are poisons, and nothing is without poison. Only the dose makes a thing not a poison.

—PARACELSUS

We now have several types of potent alchemical medicines: tinctures, magistries, *ens*, and stones. They are taken according to planetary rulership of the plant, the day, and the hour. The full use of these herbal preparations as medicines is a topic far beyond the scope of this book. The proper use can be studied in the works of Nicholas Culpeper (1616–1654). A close and careful study of Culpeper's *A Physical Directory, or a Translation of the London Dispensary*, his 1649 English translation of the *Pharmacopoeia Londonesis*, as well as his 1653 herbal *The English Physitian*, will provide a good background within which to study alchemical medicines, their preparation, and use. He provides some rules of thumb in choosing which herbs are most useful by considering the patient's astrological chart.

1. Fortifie the Body with Herbs of the Nature of the lord of the Ascendent, 'tis no matter whether he be a Fortune or an Infortune in this case.
2. Let your Medicine be somthing Antipathetical to the lord of the sixth.
3. Let your Medicine be somthing of the Nature of the Sign ascending.
4. If the lord of the Tenth be strong, make use of his Medicines.

5. If this cannot well be, make use of the Medicines of the light of time.
6. Be sure alwaies fortifie the grieved part of the body by Sympathetical Remedies.
7. Regard the Heart, keep that upon the Wheels because the Sun is the Fountain of Life, and therefore those Universal Remedies Aurum potabile, and the Phylosophers Stone, cure all Diseases by only fortifying the Heart.

The effects of these alchemical preparations are the effects of the herb itself on the physical body, on the organs ruled by the planet that rules the herb in question. In these cases a few drops are taken in water as needed, or on the first hour of the day of the planet in question. For example, solar plants are taken on Sunday at sunrise (remember the first hour of the day is ruled by the planet ruling that day), lunar plants are taken on Monday at sunrise.

These tinctures and other preparations also have effects on more subtle levels of the body and can be used in more initiatory ways. For example, the herbal preparations of the planets, whether tinctures or magistries, may be taken in progressively increased doses starting with two drops daily in water, and building, over a course of a year, to ten drops a day. They are taken every day, cycling through the seven planets' tinctures once a week. It is important that one chooses healthful and friendly plants for this purpose. Choose herbs that will not build up toxins but instead help release the impurities and balance out those organs represented by the planets. Since these preparations used in this manner have very subtle effects, a careful recording and consideration of your dreams during this period are important.

Beyond these herbal preparations, the use of any alchemical preparation made of minerals or metals should be done with the supervision and consultation of a fully qualified doctor of medicine.

CHAPTER FOURTEEN

THE MINERAL WORK

If Heaven will it, thou shalt know that Nature,
Alike in everything, is the same in every place.

—GOLDEN VERSES OF PYTHAGORAS

Alchemy has been referred to in places as terrestrial astronomy, as in Edward Kelly's *Theatre of Terrestrial Astronomy.* It is the study of the "terrestrial planets," that is, the seven metals. Much of alchemy especially from the mid-sixteenth century on was preoccupied with the concept of Three Principles and the seven "powers," i.e., the planets.

The mineral kingdom can be analyzed in terms of the Three Principles as was done with plants. Paracelsus stated, "Know that all the seven metals are born from a threefold matter, namely, Mercury, Sulphur, and Salt, but with distinct and peculiar colorings. . . . Mercury is the Spirit, Sulphur is the Soul, and Salt is the body."[1]

The initial work is opening the metal and preparing it for marriage into the plant world (the intermediary to the animal world) thereby transmuting it for human use.

The first step in this process is the calcination of the metal. Calcination is the roasting of the crushed ore just below its melting point, exposing it to air to create the oxide of the metal (also a salt of the metal). The calcination of gold, however, is done by another method. Once the metal is calcined and turned into its calx, it is then ready to be opened further. John French, in his *Art of Distillation,* states that, "they must first be reduced into salts, for then they are no more dead bodies, but by this preparation have obtained a new life, and are the metals of Philosophers."[2] This is achieved through what have been called the stone dragons, that is, the spirits of mineral salts.

The Stone Dragons: Spirits or Oils of Salts

The mineral salts that are of interest to us here are sea salt (sodium chloride), sal ammoniac (ammonium chloride), saltpeter (potassium nitrate), and vitriols (sulphates). Vitriols[56] are the sulphate salts of, most commonly, copper, iron, aluminum, and zinc. The most common are blue, green, alum, and white vitriol respectively. Like sea salt and saltpeter, they exist as naturally occurring minerals. When these stones, such as vitriol, for example, are heated, first water, sometimes referred to as the flood or as phlegm, is given off, then an oily sharp liquid comes over. This is called oil of vitriol, known today as dilute sulphuric acid. Although oil of vitriol refers to something specific, the term "vitriol" was expanded to include other acids drawn from other mineral salts. Distilling sea salt or sal ammoniac will yield a Spirit or Oil of Salt (hydrochloric acid); saltpeter will produce a Spirit of Nitre (nitric acid); aqua fortis (strong water) is distilled from saltpeter and vitriol; and *Aqua Regia* is distilled from a mix of sea salt or sal ammoniac and saltpeter.[4]

These mineral acids were obtained by distilling a salt or a mixture of salts blended with inert matter like potters clay or guilders bole. The salt and clay are first formed into small pellets then placed in a retort and heated with a fire of the highest degree. The spirit is then forced over.

The work with metals does, at one point or another, involve these very caustic and toxic spirits, and mention is often made of them. I can only recommend attempting to distill these spirits to those with adequate training and equipment to deal with boiling and vaporizing acids. First perfect your technique and work with plants, wine, and water before considering moving on.

To obtain the salt of a metal, the metal or oxide of the metal is placed into one of the above spirits. The spirit dissolves the metal. This solution is then filtered[5] and allowed to

This engraving from the seventeenth-century Museum Hermeticum Reformatum et Amplificatum *depicts the idea of "as above, so below." We see beneath the Earth Apollo and the six muses each representing one of the planets, that is, metals.*

crystallize. When crystallization is complete, take the crystals and wash them with water. If the result is soluble, filter again and evaporate. If it is insoluble, wash, filter, and dry the crystals. You now have the particular salts of the metal you are working with. Each acid forms its own type of salt. Acetic acid yields acetates. Hydrochloric acid yields chlorides. Nitric acid yields nitrates and nitrites. Sulphuric acid yields sulphates. *Aqua Regia* tends to yield chlorides due to the presence of hydrochloric acid, a component of *Aqua Regia*. With this salt, one is now ready to begin the alchemical work. The proper preparation of the salt is where true alchemy abides.

Let us consider some alchemical work that can be done with Venus. What is done with Venus can be done, with some modifications, with the other metals. Venus is good to work with both because of the relatively low level of toxicity involved and also because of the beauty of the results. The salts of Venus are mostly greens and blues. Blue vitriol is copper sulphate and occurs naturally as the mineral bluestone. This is an excellent mineral with which to explore the techniques of crystallization. Much can be learned and realized in doing only that. Malachite, copper carbonate,[6] is another lovely mineral that is almost moss-like in color and appearance. When ground finely, it makes a green pigment. Malachite is also used in jewelry due to its beauty. Verdigris, the "green of the Greeks" is a third. It is copper acetate, a rust that forms on copper plates when they are suspended over vinegar. When its crystals are large and coarse it has a deep dark green color that lightens and shifts to blue on grinding.

What we will do here is take copper, open it, and move it up, so to speak, from metal to mineral, through the vegetable, thus making it accessible to the animal realm for use perhaps as a medicine or as a precursor for a medicine.

One can start with copper metal[7] and immerse it in Oil of Vitriol, diluted sulphuric acid. This will dissolve the copper, making a blue solution of copper sulphate, moving Venus from metal to mineral. The change is very dramatic. One can also start with blue vitriol itself, since it is easier to begin the work with the mineral. If you can find it as its natural mineral bluestone, this is by far the best way to work. This is, however, one of those cases in which you can use the chemical copper sulphate to study the process and theory while you are hunting down some bluestone.

Take bluestone or copper sulphate and dissolve it in heated distilled water, as much as the water will take. Prepare a separate solution of Salt of Tartar by taking approximately an equal amount of Salt of Tartar and dissolving it in the same volume of water needed for the copper sulphate solution. Then add, little by little, the copper sulphate solution to the tartar solution, stirring constantly. A green-blue precipitate appears immediately, forming a sponge-like mass. This is green verditer, or copper carbonate, the man-made form of malachite developed in the fifteenth century. Keep stirring and adding the copper solution to the tartar solution. Filter and wash the precipitate until the runoff is neutral and shows a pH of 7 on a pH paper strip. This may take four to six washings. The longer you wait to wash the filtrate, the darker the verditer becomes. Sometimes temperature also influences the final color. The color varies from green to blue. It is very easy to get some form of green, but to get it to form the blue verditer (man-made azurite) is very tricky.

We now have moved the copper from the mineral to the first stage of the vegetable kingdom, via its salt, to the carbonate. This can be used as a pigment, or we can continue to move up the ladder. Take this green-blue powder and slowly add distilled vinegar. It will fizz as the acid reacts with the carbonate, quickly releasing carbon dioxide. This will make a very deep green solution of verdigris (copper acetate). Crystallize the solution to get verdigris.

Verdigris may also be made by suspending copper plates over warm distilled vinegar.[8] This method opens copper up directly into the animal realm. This is perfectly fine. However, making verdigris from the carbonate of copper (malachite or verditer) allows one to move copper from the realm of metals through the mineral realm and finally into the vegetable realm. In this method, with each jump and crystallization or formation, the copper is purified and opened more and more. This process does not so much transmute copper, as it does transfigure it, creating a channel through which the energies of copper may flow from the realm of metals into the vegetable realm, and in this way making it accessible to the animal realm.

From here, with direct practice enlivening theory, you can see that by using natural malachite and a properly prepared wine vinegar acetic acid, one could make a very rich verdigris—that is, a living energetic copper whose body has been thoroughly opened and ready for further work.

CHAPTER FIFTEEN

THE AURUM POTABILE

Regard the Heart, keep that upon the Wheels because the
Sun is the Fountain of Life, and therefore those Universal
Remedies Aurum potabile, and the Phylosophers Stone, cure
all Diseases by only fortifying the Heart.[1]

—NICHOLAS CULPEPER

The *aurum potabile* was another of the major challenges faced by the alchemists. The *aurum potabile* is a drinkable liquid form of gold. It possesses very potent healing qualities that touch the very heart of a person, effecting a cure from there. There are as many *aurum potabiles* as there are alchemists and physicians. There is no time or space in this volume to go into the wide variety of processes, but the *aurum potabile* is a very rich area for exploration.

To make the *aurum potabile,* the first question is, how does one open gold? How do you break through its shell and release its essence, its soul? This is what was attempted with the use of mineral and organic acids and other solvents. What was actually made was a very fine colloidal suspension of gold. Colloidal suspensions of gold and of silver have noted health benefits. Silver, for example, is an excellent antibacterial. It was used as such up until the 1930s, when the development of other more organic antibacterial agents, such as penicillin, became the therapy of choice. Silver is now often used in intravenous needles, where the need to suppress bacteria is high. There was also a custom among the early American settlers of putting a silver coin in a canteen of water to help keep it fresh. Colloidal gold is used in much the same way.

Aurum potabile is, according to the actual work of the alchemists, colloidal gold. But this, in the opinion of some alchemists, is not "true" alchemical *aurum potabile*. The gold has not truly been opened and its essence has not truly been released. The gold has only been divided very finely and has, as already noted, health benefits in and of itself, but is not a true *aurum potabile*.

The process in general is that a solvent is used to dissolve and hopefully open gold. Solvents such as *Aqua Regia* or metallic mercury, as is applied in wet gilding, are used to this end. Then a medium is used to extract, or lift, the gold or soul of gold, out of the toxic matrix of the solution. Some processes then use yet another more palatable medium into which they extract the gold once more in preparation for human consumption. This then is the *aurum potabile*.

CHAPTER SIXTEEN

Opus Magnum

The *Opus Magnum* is the Great Work. I will keep my comments on this topic brief, not having attempted this work myself. Some aspects of it, yes, I've done. But the work itself? No. However, I will present a brief overview of two methods that look very interesting.

They have come to be known as the wet way and the dry way.[1]

The wet way works with solutions and the soluble salts of the metals and was described by Sir George Ripley in his *Bosom Book of Sir George Ripley*. The dry way is the method used and described by Nicholas Flamel and clearly explicated by Eireneaus Philalethes in his *An Open Entrance to the Closed Palace of the King* and was worked with a great deal of transparency and intellectual rigor by both Sir Robert Boyle and Sir Isaac Newton.

From Museum Hermeticum Reformatum et Amplificatum.
1678.

The method laid out by Sir George Ripley follows this broadest outline. Antimony or lead is prepared and then made into an acetate salt with distilled vinegar. This salt is then dry distilled. A volatile white vapor comes over and condenses into a very volatile liquid. This is the Mercury. Distillation continues and a reddish oil comes over. This is the Sulphur. The Salt remains behind. The Salt is calcined and purified, and the other principles are joined to the Salt. It is then sealed in a flask and heated. This then goes through various stages, the end result of which is the Philosopher's Stone, which is able to transmute base metals into gold and can cure all diseases.

In the method developed by Eirenaeus Philalethes, antimony again plays a central role, but in the metallic form this time. Regulus of antimony is extracted from stibnite, an antimony ore, and purified to form a Star Regulus. This Regulus is then joined with copper or silver to further purify the Regulus, as well as to impart a part of their character to the "water" that is antimony. This highly purified antimony is then used to cleanse ordinary mercury and to make it philosophical. Ferment of gold is added to this philosophical Mercury which is then sealed into a thick flask and heated. The matter goes through various color changes and states. The end result is, like the above process, the Philosopher's Stone, or more accurately, the red powder of projection which is the form it takes in most of the transmutation stories.

To accomplish this Great Work, so much depends on the alchemist and each individual's inner preparation. There is little that I can add except that you should work within the tradition in which you are most at home, find its esoteric heart, and the points of contact it makes with alchemy, and start there.

CHAPTER SEVENTEEN

A PARTING CONTEMPLATION

On Transmutation

With your mind steadily and calmly focused, divide matter using whatever system is the most familiar, whether contemporary physics or the elements of the Greeks. Take an object and divide it. Keep dividing it with your mind until you cannot divide anymore. Enter there, rest your mind there, and begin to explore. Staying there, look around for the object with which you began. Does it really exist? Once you have brought the object to a point where it has been broken apart one step too many and been "lost," you have arrived at the point at which transmutation becomes a possibility. Is this the prima materia?

"exeunt omnium in mysterium"[1]

Some Random Thoughts and a Poem in Lieu of a Conclusion

What I have presented is a very brief condensed outline of the alchemical path. Many gates and side paths have been pointed out, and some names have been dropped. There are many possibilities for further work. The alchemical path is an extremely demanding yet fruitful endeavor able to give something to everyone—the mystic, the scholar, the philosopher, the artist, the madman, and, of course, the beloved fool. It is now time to reread and pick up some of the threads that will guide you through this labyrinth. It is important to examine the world with your own eyes, verify things with your own experience. Persist and follow the dictum *ora, lege, lege, lege, relege, labora et invenies.* It truly is the method of alchemy. But most important to make progress on the alchemical path is your motivation for pursuing alchemy. Aim it toward the benefit of others. Aim toward anything else and you run the risk of becoming seriously lost.

I include here a fragment from the *Tarjuman al-ashwaq*, a collection of mystical Odes by the great Islamic theosophist ibn al-'Arabi, as something to aspire to and necessary to the Great Work:

> *O marvel! a garden amidst fires!*
> *My heart has become capable of every form:*
> *It is a pasture for gazelles*
> *And a convent for Christian monks,*
> *And a temple for idols and the pilgrims Ka'ba*
> *And the tables of the Torah and the book of the Koran.*
> *   I follow the religion of Love:*
> *Whatever way Love's camels take,*
> *That is my religion and my faith.[2]*

Not revealed in the books, but in the practice.

APPENDICES

Technique and Equipment

Laboratory Safety

It's all fun and games until someone loses an eye.

—Mom

Two general rules of safety:

Know the theory before attempting the practice.

Before beginning any experiment it is of the utmost importance to know thoroughly what we are going to do, how we plan to do it, and what results we are expecting. The experiment should be able to be performed mentally from the beginning to its completion. This practice not only produces a safer laboratory and more efficient operation but also strengthens and develops the ability to visualize and concentrate.

When in doubt, do not do it.

There is a degree of risk in any experimental undertaking; it is the nature of experiment. But it is the purpose of experimental technique not only to give "a way into" an unknown substance, situation, or event but also to minimize the hazards that may be involved with or result from the experiment.

Some basic safety points:

1. Prepare in depth before starting any experiment.

2. Know the properties of the substances being worked with. An excellent source of this information is *The Merck Index* or *CRC of Chemistry and Physics*.

3. Never mix substances "just to see what happens." It can be a very dangerous practice, or, at the least, a waste of materials.

4. Safety or prescription glasses should be worn at all times to protect the eyes; contact lenses are inadequate.

5. Adequate footwear should be worn and long hair confined. A pair of gloves is also recommended when working with acids, bases, or toxic substances that can be absorbed through the skin, such as antimony.

6. Never eat, drink, or smoke while working in the lab.

7. When noting the odor of anything, do not stick your nose over it and sniff, but rather waft the odors to your nose with your hand.

8. When diluting acids or bases, the acid or base should always be added to the water. This reduces the risk of chemical burns from splashing.

9. Use a towel when inserting or removing glass tubing or thermometers into or out of rubber stoppers or rubber tubing. Also use water to lubricate the rubber.

10. Never heat flammable liquids with an open flame, or when any open flame is near.

11. Check and recheck all connections of a setup.

12. Always keep a charged all-purpose fire extinguisher handy in the laboratory or workplace.

13. Always have a source of fresh cold running water available in case of burns (both chemical and heat). To flush the eyes, slightly warm water is preferred. It is also a good idea to have a first aid kit available.

14. Be careful with hot glassware and metal rings—sometimes they appear the same as when cold.

15. Label things clearly with indelible ink.

16. Keep the laboratory or workplace well ventilated at all times.

17. Do not work on days when you are in a "bad mood," not feeling well, etc. Try not to push things when you feel yourself becoming fatigued. Months of work could be lost in a matter of seconds due to one small accident.

18. Think and use your common sense.

In the begining work, such as the preparation of spagyric tinctures, a lot of these rules are not strictly applicable. However, it is very important to make a habit of observing safety procedures so that they become second nature to us, and a part of our experimental repertoire.

Equipment

This is a basic list of what is needed; as you work you will add to it.

For distillation:
Flasks
Adapters
Condensors
Thermometer
Oil separator
Aludel
Clamps
Stands
Rubber tubing
Electric heat source

For calcination:
Stainless steel pans
Ceramic casserole dishes
Screens
Crucibles
Any heat source

For measurement:
Scales—mass
Graduated cylinders—volume
Thermometers—temperature
Hydrometer—liquid density
pH paper—acidity

Heat sources:
Sun
Dung
Incubator
Hot plate
Heating mantle
Bunsen burner
Stove
Oven
Open charcoal fire

Miscellaneous:
Beakers
Funnels
Filter paper
Motar and pestle
Glass stirring rods
Clamps and stands and other
    hardware
Silicon stopcock grease
Various utensils
An assortment of glass jars,
    bottles, and jugs
Cleaning supplies

Safety:
Gloves
Fire extinguisher
Eye protection
Proper disposal system
First aid kit

Laboratory Techniques

For more on laboratory techniques consult an organic chemistry laboratory manual.

Distillation

The glassware used in distillation and in other applications are basically two types: one is a glassware that uses glass tubing, rubber stoppers, and rubber hosing for connections; the other has ground glass-joints, and everything fits together very easily.

The heat source should be an electric hot plate or heating mantle where you are distilling alcohol or other flammables. Never use an open flame or have one nearby when distilling flammables.

SIMPLE DISTILLATION APPARATUS

Ground glass-jointed equipment:

- Round distilling flask
- Vacuum adapter
- Distilling head
- Round bottom flask
- Thermometer adapter
- Clamps
- Stands
- Thermometer
- Condenser and tubes
- Heat source

Standard glassware equipment:

- Rubber stoppers and glass tubing
- Distilling flask and one-holed rubber stopper (for thermometer), or
- Distilling flask and a two-holed rubber stopper (for thermometer and bent glass tube)
- Thermometer

- Receiving flask
- Heat source
- Condenser, hoses, and a one-holed rubber stopper
- Clamps and stands

Assemble the apparatus as shown in Figure 6a, 6b, or 6c on the following page. The distillation flask, condenser, and the vacuum adapter should all be clamped to stands. If using ground glass joints, lightly coat the joints with stopcock grease[66] before assembling the parts. The joints should be clear and transparent and without any bubbles. They should be checked occasionally for tightness during the distillation to prevent loss of vapor. The flask should be filled no more than two-thirds. More than this and the liquid may splash into the condenser. Less than two-thirds and too much vapor must fill the flask first before it is forced through the condenser. Insert the thermometer so that the bulb or the immersion line etched on the thermometer is just below the side arm of the distilling head (or the side arm of the distilling flask). The bulb must be in the vapor stream in order to have a correct temperature reading. Connect the water lines so that the water flows in at the bottom and exits at the top, allowing the condenser to fill with water. Put one or two boiling chips into the liquid before heating—this will prevent superheating and "bumping." Do not add the boiling chips after you have begun heating because the liquid may be superheated and to add a boiling chip too may cause the liquid to boil all at once, causing an explosion or, at the very least, violent frothing. Each time you stop boiling, you must add a new boiling chip. When the boiling point of the liquid is reached, a ring of condensate will move up through the apparatus. When it contacts the thermometer, there will be a rapid rise in temperature. The condensate will then pass through the condenser and into the receiver. At this point the distillation begins. Adjust the heat to a proper take-off rate—about one drop per second is good. Too large a take-off and equilibrium is not established and

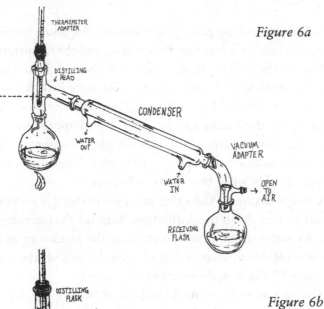

Figure 6a

THERMOMETER
ADAPTER

DISTILLING
HEAD

CONDENSER

WATER
OUT

VACUUM
ADAPTER

WATER
IN

OPEN
TO
AIR

RECEIVING
FLASK

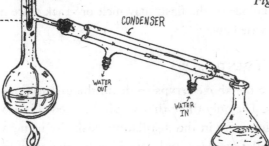

Figure 6b

DISTILLING
FLASK

CONDENSER

WATER
OUT

WATER
IN

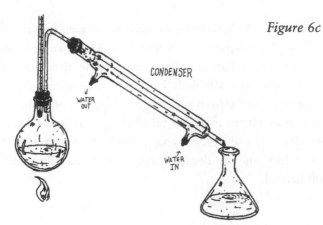

Figure 6c

CONDENSER

WATER
OUT

WATER
IN

the separation will be poor. Too slow, and the temperature is not maintained by a constant vapor flow, and the temperature reading of the boiling temperature will be too low. Traditionally, the time between drops was the time it took to say one *Pater noster,* the Lord's Prayer. Once the temperature is adjusted, the distillation can be allowed to happen. Keep an eye on the temperature; it will indicate when the next component of the solution is about to come over. The temperature will rise quickly when this starts to happen.

Change receivers. And either continue to distill if necessary or start to shut down the distillation. Turn off the heat and let the cold water continue to run through the condenser as the system cools down. Once it is cool enough, turn off the water and carefully begin to disassemble the setup.

One last note: Never distill to dryness because the dry residue may explode or the flask may melt or crack since heat is not being carried away.

To Distill Essential Oils

One can use the above setups to distill the essential oil from dried herbs. The only thing that would be needed is a way to replenish the water in the distillation flask. By using a two-necked distillation flask and attaching a separation funnel, water can be added during the distillation without interrupting it.

Water and the herb to be distilled are placed into the flask and allowed to macerate for a few days. More water is added just before the distillation to bring the volume up to it previous level. The setup is assembled. The cold water is turned on and then the heat. As the herb and solution begin to boil, the steam vapor carries off the essential oil of the plant. A good way to collect this is to collect the water and oil into a separation funnel. As it fills, one can drain off the water from below, leaving the oil behind.

Alternatively one can use an oil separator, which, by a system of valves, allows the water to siphon back into the flask or the oil to be drained off. It is very easy and convenient to use.

APPENDIX 2

PLANTS AND PLANETS

THE PLANT KINGDOM IS ALSO related to the heavens, with each plant having a planetary ruler. In general, there are three basic systems to determine planetary rulership. They can be called: the mythic, the functional, and the doctrine of signatures.

The Mythic: plants as they relate to the gods of Roman and Greek mythology as well as folklore.

The Functional: the effects plants have on the body and the planetary rulership of the part of the body affected.

The Doctrine of Signatures: the form, color, and/or habitat of the plant as related to the planets.

The following tables of rulership, drawn from Nicholas Culpeper and William Lilly (1602–1681), are not to be followed slavishly, but with thought and consideration as to the ultimate use of the plant.

Saturn

NAME	LATIN NAME
Amaranth	*Amaranthus hypochondriacas*
Angelica	*Angelica archangelica*
Black elder	*Sambucus nigra*
Blackthorn, Sloe, White plum	*Prunus spinosa*
Box	*Buxus sempervirens*
Buckthorn	*Rhamnus catharticus, Rhamnus frangula*
Corn	*Zea mays*
Cornflower, Blue bottle	*Centaurea cyanus*
Cypress tree	*Cypressus*
Fenugreek, Bird's foot	*Foenum graecum*
Flax	*Linum usitatissimum*
Hemp	*Cannabis sativa*
Horsetail	*Equisetum arvense*
Mandrake	*Mandragora officinarum*
Nightshade, Bittersweet	*Solanum dulcamara*
Nightshade, Black	*Solanum nigrum*
Nightshade, Deadly	*Atropa belladonna*
Quince tree	*Cydonia vulgaris*
Solomon's seal	*Polygonatm multiflorum*
Wintergreen	*Gaultheria procumbens*
Woad	*Isatis tinctoria*
Yew	*Taxus baccata*

Jupiter

NAME	LATIN NAME
Arnica	*Arnica Montana*
Ash	*Fraxinus excelsior*
Balm, Lemon	*Melissa officinalis*
Betony, Wood	*Betonica officinalis*
Bilberry	*Vaccinum myrtillus*
Borage	*Borago officinalis*
Comfrey	*Symphytum officinale*
Dandelion	*Taraxacum officinalis*
Dock, Yellow	*Rumex crispus*
Fig tree	*Figus carica*
Flax	*Linum usitatissimum*
Ginseng	*Panax ginseng*
Hyssop	*Hysopus officinale*
Jasmine	*Jasminum officinale*
Jimsonweed	*Datura stramonium*
Juniper	*Juniperus communis*
Laurel, Bay	*Laurus nobilis*
Mistletoe	*Viscum album*
Mullein, White	*Verbasum thapisforme*
Myrrh	*Commiphora myrrha*
Oak	*Quecus robur*
Oats	*Avena sativa*
Olive	*Olea europaea*
Oregano	*Origanum vulgare*
Sage	*Salvia officinalis*

Mars

Name	Latin Name
Aloe	*Aloe spp*
Barberry	*Berberis vulgaris*
Basil	*Ociniam basilicum*
Box	*Buxus sempervirens*
Bryony, Red	*Bryonia dioica*
Buttercup	*Ranuculus bulbosus*
Catnip	*Nepeta cataria*
Cayenne, Peppers	*Capisicum frutescens*
Chive	*Allium schoenoprasum*
Coriander	*Coriandrum sativum*
Dwarf elder	*Sambucus ebulus*
Flax, Linseed	*Linum usitatissimum*
Garlic	*Allium sativum*
Hawthorn	*Crataegus oxyacanthus*
Honeysuckle	*Lonicera caprifolium*
Hops	*Humulus lupulus*
Horseradish	*Arnoracia lapathefolis*
Madder	*Rubia tinctoum*
Mustard	*Brassica nigra*
Mustard, all	*Sinapis*
Nettle	*Uratica dioica*
Oak	*Quercus robur*
Onion	*Allium cepa*
Parsley	*Petroselinum crispum*
Radish	*Raphanus sativus*
Thistles	*Cirsium spp*
Tobacco	*Nicotiana tabacum*
Wild lettuce	*Lactuca virosa*

Sun

Name	Latin Name
Calamus	Calamus aromaticus
Cedar	Cedrus deodara,Cedrus libani
Celandine, Greater	Chelidonium majus
Centaury, Small	Centaurium cyanus, Erythrea centaurium
Chamomile, Roman	Anthemis nobilis, Matricaria chamomile
Chamomille, German	Matricaria chamomilla
Cinnamon	Cinnamonum ceylanicum
Elecampane	Inula helenium
Eyebright	Euphrasia officinalis
Frankincense	Boswellia sacra
Ginger	Zingiber officinale
Grapevine	Vitis vinifera
Juniper	Juniperus communis
Laurel	Laurus nobilis
Lemon balm	Melissa officinalis
Marigold	Calendula officinalis
Mistletoe	Viscum album
Passionflower	Passiflora incarnata
Peony	Paeonia officinalis
Plantain	Plantago major
Rose damask	Rosa damascena
Rosemary	Rosemarius officinalis
Rue	Ruta graveolens
Saffron	Crocus sativus
St. John's wort	Hypericum perforatum
Sundew	Drosera rotundifolia
Sunflower	Helianthus anuus

Venus

Name	Latin Name
Almonds	*Prunus dulcis*
Birch	*Betula alba*
Blackberry	*Rubus villosus*
Boneset	*Eupatorium perfoliatum*
Buckthorn	*Rhanus frangula*
Bugloss	*Anchusa officinalis*
Burdock	*Arctium lappa*
Catnip	*Nepeta cataria*
Elder	*Sambucus nigra*
Feverfew	*Chrysanthenum parthenium*
Figwort	*Scrophularia nodosa*
Foxglove, Digitalis	*Digitalis purpurea*
Lady's mantle	*Alchimilla vulgaris*
Marshmallow	*Althea officinalis*
Mint, all	*Mentae spp.*
Mugwort	*Artemisia vulgaris*
Rose	*Rosa damascena*
Sanicle	*Sanicula, spp.*
Thyme	*Thymus vulgaris*
Valerian	*Valeriana officinalis*
Vervain	*Verbena officinalis*
Violet	*Viola odorata*
Yarrow	*Alchilea millefolium*

Mercury

NAME	LATIN NAME
Byrony	*Bryonia alba*
Calamint	*Calamintha officinalis or arvenis*
Caraway	*Carum carvi*
Carrot	*Daucus carota*
Celery	*Apium graveolens*
Cubeb pepper	*Piper cubeba*
Dill	*Anethum graveolens*
Elecampane	*Inula hellenium*
Endive, Chicory	*Chicorium endiva*
Fennel	*Foeniculum vulgare*
Fenugreek	*Trigonella foenum-grecum*
Flax	*Linum usitatissimum*
Foxglove	*Digitalis purpurea*
Hazelnut	*Corylus, spp.*
Honeysuckle	*Lonicera caprifolium*
Lavender	*Lavendula officinalis or vera*
Licorice	*Glycyrrahiza glnbra*
Marjoram, Sweet	*Majorana hortensis*
Mulberry, White and Black	*Morus, spp. Alba and nigra*
Myrtle	*Myrtus communis*
Oats	*Avena sativa*
Oregano	*Origanum vulgare*
Parsley	*Petroselinum hortense*
Savory	*Satureia hortensis*
Valerian	*Valeriana officinalis*
Vervain	*Verbena simplex*
Wormwood	*Artemisia absinthium*

Moon

Name	Latin Name
Acanthus	*Acanthus mollis*
Adder's tongue	*Erthronium americanum*
Clary sage	*Salvia sclarea*
Cleavers	*Galium aparine*
Daisy	*Bellis perennis*
Hyssop	*Hyssopus officinalis*
Iris, var	*Iris var.*
Lettuce, Common	*Lactuca sativa*
Lime tree or Linden tree	*Tilia cordata*
Mandrake	*Mandragora officinalis*
Mushrooms	
Myrtle, Periwinkle	*Vinca minor*
Nutmeg	*Myristica fragans*
Poppy, Corn	*Papaver rhoeas*
Poppy, Opium	*Papaver somniferum*
Pumpkin	*Cucurbita Pepo*
Sassafras	*Sassafras albidum*
Saxifrage	*Saxifraga tridactyles*
Turmeric	*Curcuma longa*
Veronica, Speedwell	*Veronica officinalis*
Water lily	*Nymphaea alba*
Watercress	*Nasturtium officinalis*
White lily	*Lilium candicum* or *album*
Willows	*Salix. Alba, nigra, caprea*

BIBLIOGRAPHY

THE FOLLOWING IS A SHORT LIST of useful texts for those who wish to go further with the work. Many of the primary texts are now available online, and a simple search on the name of the author or title will lead you to some remarkable resources. I highly recommend The Alchemy website *www.levity.com/ alchemy/home.html*. It has a vast wealth of information and primary sources.

History

al-Hasan, Ahmad. *Islamic Technology*. 1986. Cambridge University Press. London.

Burckhardt, Titus. *Alchemy: Science of the Cosmos, Science of the Soul*. 1967. Stuart & Watkins. London.

Dobbs, Betty Jo Teeter. *The Foundations of Newton's Alchemy*. 1983. Cambridge University Press. Cambridge.

Eliade, Mircea. *The Forge and the Crucible*. 1978. Trans. Stephen Corrin. University of Chicago Press. Chicago.

———*Yoga: Immortality and Freedom*. 1958. Bollingen Foundation, Pantheon Books. New York.

Florensky, Pavel. *Iconostasis*. 2000. Trans. Donald Sheehan and Olga Andrejev. St. Vladimir's Seminary Press. New York.

Hartmann, Franz. *The Life of Philippus Theophrastus, Bombast of Hohenheim*. 1887. G. Redway. London.

Holmyard, E. J. *Alchemy*. 1957. Penguin Books. England.

Klossowski de Rola, Stanislas. *The Golden Game*. 1996. Thames and Hudson. New York.

Lindsay, Jack. *The Origins of Alchemy in Graeco-Roman Egypt*. 1970. Fredrik Muller Ltd. London.

Roob, Alexander. *Alchemy and Mysticism*. 2001. Taschen. Cologne.

Sendler, Egon. *The Icon, Image of the Invisible*. 1988. Trans. Fr. Steven Bigham. Oakwood Publications. California.

Wasserman, James. *Art and Symbols of the Occult.* 1993. Revised and expanded edition retitled *The Mystery Traditions.* 2005. Destiny Books. Vermont.

Yates, Francis A. *The Art of Memory.* 1966. University of Chicago Press. Chicago.

Alchemy

Agrippa, Henry Cornelius. *The Books of Occult Philosophy. Book II.* 1998. Ed. Donald Tyson. Llewellyn Publications. Minnesota.

Albertus, Frater. 1975. *The Alchemist's Handbook.* 1974. Samuel Weiser, Inc. New York.

Albertus Magnus. *The Compound of Compounds.* 2003. Trans. Luc Villeneuve. Hermetic Research Series No. 14. Glasgow.

——*Libellus de alchimia.* 1958. Trans. Sister Virginia Heines, S.C.N. University of California Press.

Allen, Paul M. *A Christian Rosenkreutz Anthology.* 1974. Rudolph Steiner Publications. New York

Ashmole, Elias. *Theatrum chemicum Britannicum.* 1968. Georg Olms Verlags-buchhandlung. Hildesheim.

Barbault, Armand. *Gold of a Thousand Mornings.* 1975. Neville Spearman. London.

Bernus, Alexander von. *Médecine et alchimie.* 1977. Belfond. Paris.

Boehme, Jacob. *The Signature of All Things.* 1969. James Clarke & Co. Cambridge.

Boyle, Robert. *The Work Diary of Robert Boyle.* 1655. Published at *www.bbk.ac.uk/boyle/workdiaries/*

Cockren, Archibald. *Alchemy Rediscovered and Restored.* 1941. David McKay Co. Philadelphia.

Collectanea Chemica. 1963. Vincent Stuart Publishers. London.

Flamel, Nicolas. *Nicholas Flamel: His Exposition of the Hieroglyphicall Figures.* 1994. Garland Publishing, Inc. New York.

French, John. *The Art of Distillation.* 1651. Richard Cotes. London.

Geber. *The Alchemical Works of Geber.* 1994. Trans. Richard Russel. Samuel Weiser, Inc. Maine.

Glaser, Christophe. *The Complete Chemist.* 1677. Reprinted Kessinger Publishing Co. Montana.

Helmont, Johann van. *Ortus Medicinae.* 1952. Amsterdam.

Hermetic Museum, The. Two volumes in one. 1999. Edited and trans. A. E. Waite. Samuel Weiser, Inc. Maine.

Jacobi, Jolande. *Paracelsus.* 1979. Princeton University Press. New Jersey.

Jong, H.M.E. de. *Michael Maier's Atalanta Fugiens.* 2002. Nicolas-Hays, Inc. Maine.

Junius, Manfred M. *Practical Handbook of Plant Alchemy.* 1985. Inner Traditions International. New York.

Maier, Michael. *Atalanta fugiens.* 1618. 1964 reprint Im Barenreiter Verlag Kassel und Basel.

Morienus. *The Book of the Composition of Alchemy.* 2002. Hermetic Research Series No. 10. Glasgow. A 17th century English translation of *Liber de compositione alchimiae.* A translation of *The Epistle of Maryanus, the Hermit and Philosopher to Prince Khalid ibn Yazid.*

——A Testament of Alchemy. 1974. Trans. Lee Stavenhagen. Brandeis University Press. A translation of *The Epistle of Maryanus, the Hermit and Philosopher to Prince Khalid ibn Yazid.*

Pancaldi, Augusto. *Alchimia Pratica.* 1997. Atanor. Rome.

Paracelsus. *The Hermetic and Alchemical Writings of Aureolus Philippus Theophrastus Bombast, of Hohenheim, called Paracelsus the Great. 2 Vols.* 1967. Edited and trans. A. E. Waite. University Books Inc. New York.

Pernety, Antoine-Joseph. *Dictionnaire Mytho-Hermetique.* 1758. 1980 reprint. Arche Milano, Paris.

Petrus of Ferrara Bonus. *The New Pearl of Great Price.* 1974. Arno Press. New York.

Philalethes, Eirenaeus. *Alchemical Works: Eirenaeus Philalethes Compiled.* 1994. Edited S. Merrow Broddle. Cinnabar. Colorado.

Ripley, George. *The Compound of Alchymy.* 1977. Walter J. Johnson, Inc. New Jersey.

Ruland, Martin. *A Lexicon of Alchemy.* 1984. Trans. A. E. Waite. Samuel Weiser, Inc. Maine.

Trismosin, Salomon. *Splendor Solis.* 1991. Trans. Joscelyn Godwin. Phanes Press. Michigan.

Urbigerus, Baro. *Circulatum minus Urbigeranum.* 1690. 1973 reprint. Golden Manuscripts Para Publishing Co. Inc. Salt Lake City, Utah.

Valentine, Basil. *Last Will and Testament.* 1993. English Grand Lodge AMORC. California.

——*The Triumphal Chariot of Antimony.* 1962. Vincent Stuart Ltd. London.

Weidenfeld, Johannes Segerus. *Concerning the Secrets of the Adepts.* 1694. Reprinted Kessinger Publishing. Montana.

Zosimos. *Les Alchimistes Grecs. Zosime de Panopolis.* 1995. Ed. and trans. Michele Mertens. Les Belles Lettres. Paris.

Astrology

Barton, Tamsyn. *Ancient Astrology.* 1995. Routledge, New York.

Lilly, William. *Christian Astrology.* 2005. Ed. David R. Roell. Astrology Classics. Maryland.

Lineman, Rose and Jan Popelka. *Compendium of Astrology.* 1984. Whitford Press. Pennsylvania.

Michelsen, Neil F. *The American Ephemeris for the 21st Century 2000 to 2050.* 2001. ACS Publications, California.

Ptolemy. *Tetrabiblos.* 1994. Trans. F. E. Robbins. Loeb Classical Library. Harvard University Press.

Simotta, George. *A Theater of The Planetary Houres For All Dayes of the Year. 1631.* 1971 Reprint. Da Capo Press. New York.

Medicine

Avicenna. *The Canon of Medicine.* 1999. Adapted by Laleh Bakhtiar. Great Books of the Islamic World. Chicago.

Culpeper, Nicholas. *Culpeper's Complete Herbal.* [1923]. Foulsham & Co. London.

Green, James. *The Herbal Medicine-Maker's Handbook.* 2000. Crossing Press. California.

Grieve, Mrs. M. *A Modern Herbal.* 1998. Cresset Press. Twickenham.

Tobyn, Graeme. *Culpeper's Medicine: A Practice of Western Holistic Medicine.* 1977. Element Books. Great Britain.

Philosophy and Theology

Aristotle. *De Generatione et Corruptione.* 1982. Trans. with notes C. J. F. Williams. Clarendon Press. Oxford.

———*Metaphysics.* 1960. Trans. Richard Hope. University of Michigan Press.

———*Meteorology.* 1987. Trans. H.D.P. Lee. Loeb Classical Library, Harvard University Press.

———*On The Heavens.* 2000. Trans. W.K.C. Gutherie. Loeb Classical Library, Harvard University Press.

———*Physics.* 1999. Trans. Robin Waterfield. Oxford University Press. Oxford.

Bobik, Joseph. *Aquinas on Matter and Form and the Elements. A Translation and Interpretation of the* De Principiis Naturae

and the De Mixtione Elementorum *of St. Thomas Aquinas.*
1998. University of Notre Dame Press, Indiana.

Guthrie, W.K.C. *A History of Greek Philosophy. The Presocratic
Tradition from Parmenides to Democritus.* 2000. Cambridge University Press. Cambridge.

Heisenberg,Werner. *Physics and Philosophy: The Revolution in
Modern Science.* 1962. Harper and Row. New York.

Nag Hammadi Library, The. 1990. Ed. James M. Robinson. Harper.
San Francisco.

Nasr, Seyyed Hossein. *An Introduction to Islamic Cosmological Doctrines.* 1993. SUNY Press. Albany.

Nikodimos, St.: St. Makarios. *The Philokalia.* 1983. Trans. G.E.H.
Palmer, Philip Sherrard, Kallistos Ware. Faber and Faber.
London.

Plato. *Timaeus and Critias.* Trans. Desmond Lee. 1977. Penguin
Books. New York.

Pseudo-Dionysus. *Pseudo-Dionysus. The Complete Works.* 1987.
Trans. Colm Luibheid. Paulist Press. The Mystical
Theology.

Schimmel, Annemarie. *Mystical Dimensions of Islam.* 1975. University of North Carolina Press. Chapel Hill.

van den Broek, Roelof and Wouter J. Hanegraaff. *Gnosis and Hermeticism from Antiquity to Modern Times.* 1998. State
University of New York Press. New York.

Wallace, B. Alan. *Choosing Reality.* 1996. Snow Lion Publications.
Ithaca, NY.

Wright, M.R. *Cosmology in Antiquity.* 1996. Routledge. London
and New York.

Technical Manuals and Reference

CRC Handbook of Chemistry and Physics. [n.d.] CRC Press. Cleveland. *Encyclopaedia Britannica* Vol 2 1771.

Fessenden, Ralph J., Joan S. Fessenden, and Patty Feist. *Organic Laboratory Techniques.* 2000. Brooks/Cole. California.

The Merck Index. [n.d.]. Merck. Rahway, NJ.

Merrifield, Mary P. *Medieval and Renaissance Treatises on the Arts of
Painting.* 1999. Dover Publications. New York.

Theophilus. *On Divers Arts.* 1979. Trans. John Hawthorne and Cyril
Stanley Smith. Dover Publications. New York.

NOTES TO THE TEXT

Preface

1 Alchemy and iconography have similar origins. Both practices have roots in Egypt (ca. 500 B.C.) and were developed and used by Christianized Greeks in Alexandria. Icons were initially sarcophagus paintings, that is, the painting of the deceased's portrait on the coffin itself. Icon writing developed from there. However, instead of idealized portraits of the deceased, we have idealized symbolic portraits of Jesus, the Holy Family, saints, angels, and events of the Bible.

The materials used in iconography are a wood base, cloth, marble gesso, tempera, and mineral pigments. The process of painting is done in stages beginning with an empty field of white. The image is built up, layer upon layer, first of chaos, and then, with use of lighter and lighter pigments, a form rises and takes shape out of the chaos. The finished icon is then sanctified and used as an object of prayer and meditation. The process incorpo-rates revelation and the ascent to light.

2 Gnosis, which comes from the Greek *gnosis* meaning "knowledge," is a belief that the direct knowledge of or union with God is possible.

Ora

1 Basil Valentine. *The Triumphal Chariot of Antimony.* 1962. Vincent Stuart Ltd. p. 12.

2 Albertus Magnus. *Libellus de alchimia.* Translated by Sister Virginia Heines. University of California Press. 1958. p. 1.

Overview of Alchemy

1 *The Alchemical Works of Geber.* 1994. Trans. by Richard Russell. Samuel Weiser. p. 4.

2 Jolande Jacobi. *Paracelsus.* 1979. Princeton University Press. p. 141.

3 Pernety, Antoine-Joseph. *Dictionnaire Mytho-Hermetique.* 1758. 1980 reprint. Arche Milano, Paris. p. 17. "L'Alchymie est une science, et l'art de faire une poudre fermentative, qui transmue les metaux imparfaits en or, et qui sert de remede universal a tous les maux naturels des hommes, des animaux et des plantes."

4 Frater Albertus. *The Alchemist's Handbook.* 1974. Samuel Weiser, Inc. p.14.

5 Jolande Jacobi. *Paracelsus.* p. 143.

6 Khalid ibn Yazid ibn Mu'awiya (ca. 668–ca.704 or 708) was a son of the sec-ond Ummayyad calif Yazid I.

Chapter One

1 Aristotle. *Metaphysics*. Book V, Part 4. Translated by W. D. Ross.

2 Werner Heisenberg. Physics and Philosophy: *The Revolution in Modern Science*. 1962. Harper and Row. p. 58.

3 Plato. *Timaeus 55*. Plato's theory of the elements was drawn from the Pythagoreans. In *Timaeus*, Plato describes the four elements in terms of the five regular geometric solids that now bear his name, the Platonic Solids. The triangle is the fundamental building block of these solids, which are: the Tetrahedron—Fire, built of three triangles; the Octahedron—Air, made of eight triangles; the Icosahedron—Water, made of twenty triangles; the Cube—Earth, made of twelve triangles or twenty-four triangles; and the Dodecahedron—Space or the Quintessence, made of sixty triangles.

4 Plato initially had greater weight in the early Middle Ages but was quickly superceded by Aristotle. Aristotle's works on natural phenomena in our cos-mos were particularly important. Plato's influence was felt again in the six-teenth century with the translation into Latin of the late antiquity Neo-Platonists. This along with the translation of the Hermetic Corpus gave a new dimension to alchemy.

5 Avicenna. *Canon of Medicine*. 1999. Adapted by Laleh Bakhtiar. *Great Books of the Islamic World*. p. 16.

6 Avicenna. *Canon of Medicine*. p. 16.

7 Avicenna. *Canon of Medicine*. p. 15.

8 Avicenna. *Canon of Medicine*. p. 15.

9 Aristotle. *Meteorology*, Book III, Part 5. Trans. E. W. Weber.

10 Albertus *Magnus. Libellus de alchimia* pp. 8–9.

11 Paracelsus. *Samtliche Werke* 3, 42f. De Mineralibus (On Minerals).

12 Antoine Joseph Pernety. *Dictionnaire Mytho-Hermetique*. p. 17. One could argue that in working with nuclear forces one is indeed working as nature works; the same forces are at work here as they are in the stars, the source, according to contemporary cosmology and physics, of our elements.

13 Today the first point of Aries is located at 24° Pisces and moves at the rate of 50.3 arc seconds per year. This is due to the fact that the Earth, in addition to its rotation on its axis, has an additional movement in which the actual axis rotates very slowly, much like a spinning top does. It completes a full cycle in about 25,800 years, moving through one sign of the Zodiac in about 2,150 years. This is known as the precession of the equinoxes. The first point of Aries will soon align with the constellation of Aquarius, ending the Age of Pisces and bringing the dawn of the Age of Aquarius.

14 Pseudo-Dionysus. *Pseudo-Dionysus. The Complete Works*. 1987. Trans. Colm Luibheid. Paulist Press. The Mystical Theology. p. 135.

Chapter Three

1 Henry Cornelius Agrippa. *The Books of Occult Philosophy. Book II.* 1998. Ed. Donald Tyson. Llewellyn Publications. p. 371.

Chapter Five

1 The Gospel of Thomas. *The Nag Hammadi Library* 37. Ed. James M. Robinson. Harper. pp. 20–35.

2 Nicholas Flamel. 1624. *Nicholas Flamel: His Exposition of the Hieroglyphical Figures.* Translated by Eirenaeus Orandus. London. p. 10.

Chapter Six

1 This has the sense of "turned toward earth," that is, the power is being turned toward and into earth.

2 This has the sense of full intellect and superior mind, not just clever manipulation.

Chapter Seven

1 Albertus Magnus. *Compound of Compounds.* 2003. Hermetic Research Series No. 14. Trans. Luc Villeneuve. p. 8.

2 One should also consider the role that impurities might play in the process.

3 Named after its inventor, the alchemist Maria Prophetess or Maria the Jewess, third century A.D.

Chapter Eight

1 Paracelsus. *The Hermetic and Alchemical Writings of Paracelsus.* 1967. University Books. Vol. 1. p. 92.

2 This can be obtained from a wine-making supply shop.

3 A hydrometer is used to determine the concentration. This is a very simple device that looks like a short squat thermometer with a scale of densities on the side. When immersed in a solution, it sinks to a certain level and one can read the density of the liquid from the scale. When this number is checked against a chart of compounds, such as alcohol or acetic acid, you can determine the concentration as percentage.

4 Also obtained from a wine-making supply shop.

5 At 29°C to 32°C conversion takes four to six weeks; above 60°C the vinegar bacteria die.

6 Raw tartar is becoming more and more difficult to find due to the use of automated cleaning and flushing technologies to remove the residues from fermentation tanks.

Chapter Nine

1 Another method to test the concentration is to take a piece of good marble and suspend it a known volume of vinegar to be tested. When the reaction is finished and the vinegar no longer tastes sour, take the marble chip, wash, dry, and weigh it. Subtract the end weight from the starting weight of the marble. The amount of pure acetic acid in the solution is 5/6 of the weight the marble lost in the reaction.

Chapter Eleven

1 "Gur" is an essence, and since it was drawn from water, a universal substance; it is a universal essence.

2 In *Parachemy*, Spring 1977, vol. V, No. 2, p. 433, the results of an experiment with the Archaeus of Water reported that the Archaeus of Water was slightly acidic with a pH of 4.8. The final pH differed from an initial pH 5 of the rain water.

3 Robert Boyle. *The Work Diary of Robert Boyle*. 1655. BP 8 fol. 147, Item 90.

4 Basil Valentine. *The Triumphal Chariot of Antimony*. p.97.

Chapter Twelve

1 John French. *The Art of Distillation*. 1651. London. Book 1. p. 31.

2 Franz Hartmann. *The Life of Philippus Theophrastus, Bombast of Hohenheim*. 1887. G. Redway. London. p. 210.

3 Johann Van Helmont. *Ortus Medicinae*. p. 346.

4 Stirke is George Starkey who wrote under the name of Eireneaus Philalethes. Eireneaus Philalethes, considered to be one of the greatest alchemical adepts, was a teacher to Sir Robert Boyle, one of the fathers of modern chemistry.

5 To distill to dryness, you must carefully lower the heat as the liquid gets low. And as the mass approaches solid it should be kept at a warming heat to quicken its drying. The important thing is not to burn it.

6 Baro Urbigerus. *Circulatum minus Urbigeranum*. 1690. 1973 reprint. Golden Manuscripts Para Publishing Co. Inc. p. 36.

7 Resins are the insoluble secretions of trees; from these resins balsams may be obtained.

8 Also known as *pinus maritime*.

9 The essential oil of the plant is "weakened" during commercial distillation, so resin is used is to augment the strength of the oil. What is likely happening is that the resin is providing the acids that were lost in the distillation of the essential oil.

10 To make a Stone seal the circulatum in a flask and set it to digest. Start at a low heat (40°C) and then increase the heat slowly for one philosophical month (i.e., 40 days).

Chapter Fourteen

1 *The Hermetic and Alchemical Writings of Paracelsus.* Vol. 1. p. 125.

2 John French. *The Art of Distillation.* p. 193.

3 The vitriols are also known as "atraments" from the Greek *atramentum* meaning shoe black, referring to its use in dyeing leather.

4 Alternatively, three parts of Spirit of Salt and one part of Spirit of Saltpeter can also be mixed to obtain *Aqua Regia.*

5 The solution needs to be close to neutral before filtering. If it is acidic, keep heating to evaporate the solution and excess acid. As the volume decreases, keep adding fresh distilled water to maintain the original volume. Keep doing this until the solution is close to neutral. This can be tested with pH paper.

6 Azurite is another copper carbonate, but as its name implies, is a deep blue color.

7 Copper is one of the metals that can be found in its pure metallic form and is usually called "native copper."

8 Another method of preparing verdigris is to use native copper and acetic acid. When suspending sheets of copper over the acid, a green "rust" forms which is then scraped off and purified by simply redissolving it in distilled vinegar and crystallizing it. This is "distilled verdigris," or "verde eterno"

Chapter Fifteen

1 Nicholas Culpeper. *Culpeper's Complete Herbal.* [1923]. Foulsham & Co. p. 416.

Chapter Sixteen

1 The terms were originally used to describe two methods of purifying gold.

Chapter Seventeen

1 "Everything flows out into mystery." *Summa Theologia.* St. Thomas Aquinas 651978. Royal Asiatic Society, London. p. 67.

2 This is to prevent freezing and to form a seal.

ABOUT THE AUTHOR

B rian Cotnoir is an alchemist, artist and award-winning filmmaker. He is a contributor to *Parachemy: Journal of Hermetic Arts and Sciences*, the alchemical bulletin of Frater Albertus, and the author of the recently published *Emerald Tablet*, which includes his translations of and commentary on the earliest Arabic and Latin versions of this seminal alchemical text. His films have been screened at MoMA, Sundance Film Festival, HBO, PBS and other international venues.

To Our Readers

Weiser Books, an imprint of Red Wheel/Weiser, publishes books across the entire spectrum of occult, esoteric, speculative, and New Age subjects. Our mission is to publish quality books that will make a difference in people's lives without advocating any one particular path or field of study. We value the integrity, originality, and depth of knowledge of our authors.

Our readers are our most important resource, and we appreciate your input, suggestions, and ideas about what you would like to see published.

Visit our website at *www.redwheelweiser.com* to learn about our upcoming books and free downloads, and be sure to go to *www.redwheelweiser.com/newsletter* to sign up for newsletters and exclusive offers.

You can also contact us at *info@rwwbooks.com* or at

Red Wheel/Weiser, LLC
65 Parker Street, Suite 7
Newburyport, MA 01950